UNIVERSITY OF NORTH CAROLINA
STUDIES IN THE ROMANCE LANGUAGES AND LITERATURES
Number 120

FROM VULGAR LATIN TO OLD PROVENÇAL

FROM VULGAR LATIN TO OLD PROVENÇAL

BY
FREDE JENSEN

CHAPEL HILL
THE UNIVERSITY OF NORTH CAROLINA PRESS

DEPÓSITO LEGAL: V. 3.513 - 1972

ARTES GRÁFICAS SOLER, S. A. - JÁVEA, 28 - VALENCIA (8) - 1972

TO GERHARD ROHLFS

Tutti l'ammiran, tutti onor gli fanno
(DANTE)

TABLE OF CONTENTS

	Pages
PREFACE	11
PHONETIC SYMBOLS AND DIACRITICAL SIGNS	13
ABBREVIATIONS	14
BIBLIOGRAPHICAL ABBREVIATIONS	15
THE PROVENÇAL LANGUAGE	17
A BRIEF OUTLINE OF PROVENÇAL PHONOLOGY	19
THE TROUBADOUR BIOGRAPHIES	22
1. Bertran de Born	24
2. Peire Vidal	40
3. Razó (Bertran de Born: Pois lo gens terminis floris)	53
THE TROUBADOUR POETRY	79
1. Bernart de Ventadorn: Can vei la lauzeta mover	81
2. La Comtessa de Dia: A chantar m'er de so q'ieu no volria	100
3. Giraut de Bornelh: Reis glorios, verais lums e clartatz	113
BIBLIOGRAPHY	127
INDEX	132

PREFACE

In 1901, Karl Voretzsch published his famous manual, *Einführung in das Studium der altfranzösischen Sprache*, which sprang from his teaching at the University of Tübingen. The book was designed in such a way as to become a sort of "Teach Yourself" manual in Old French and owed its great success to this new pedagogical approach as well as to its factual content. Its presentation of French historical grammar through a detailed study of an Old French text has served generations of students, and its contents have recently been brought up to date (in 1955, the 8th edition) by Gerhard Rohlfs, a fact which further attests to the continued usefulness and success of the book. It is my intention, with the present work, to make Voretzsch' pedagogical approach to historical Romance linguistics available to English-speaking readers. My main inspiration, however, is drawn from Gerhard Rohlfs' admirable book, *Vom Vulgärlatein zum Altfranzösischen* (Tübingen: Niemeyer, 1960), which must have amply satisfied Whitehead's clamor (in 1952) for "a really rejuvenated Voretzsch."

Rohlfs' book contains shorter sections on Vulgar Latin, Italian and Provençal, leading up to the true *pièce de résistance*, the presentation of Old French on the basis of the study of a *lai* by Marie de France. The study of Provençal commands a total of about 30 pages, devoted to a linguistic commentary of a few prose texts drawn from the biographies of Jaufré Rudel, Peire d'Alvernhe and Giraut de Bornelh. I shall proceed somewhat differently from Rohlfs, since, in view of the amount of work that is already available in Old French and Vulgar Latin, I have chosen to make Old Provençal the sole fare. In order to achieve a more detailed picture of the linguistic conditions of the target language, I have decided not to limit my source material to the prose writings of the troubadour biographers, but to cover also a few selected poems by some of the famed troubadour poets.

The present work is intended as a manual for beginners in the field of Provençal linguistics and, perhaps more precisely, as a guidance in the linguistic interpretation of medieval Provençal texts. Since this book is conceived as a running commentary of selected pieces of literature, it cannot offer the beginner any systematic presentation of Provençal phonology, morphology, syntax or lexicography, but I feel that my selections are extensive enough to warrant adequate coverage of most major issues in these various areas. It is my hope that this presentation will give the students a taste of the great variety of problems that deserve their attention and spur them on to further readings in the field.

The most important material is presented in the main text, but additional information is given in a large number of notes which also contain references to further treatment in the various manuals and special literature available to the student.

I wish to acknowledge my obligations to M. Alain Dufour of the Librairie Droz in Geneva for his kind permission to reprint the prose and poetry selections, numbered 11, 12, 25, 28, 37 and 39, from F. Hamlin, P. T. Ricketts et J. Hathaway: *Introduction à l'Étude de l'Ancien Provençal*, Genève: Droz, 1967. I am grateful to Professor Lathrop for his sustained interest in my Romance research and for his advice and many helpful suggestions in preparing the manuscript. The scholars on whose writings I have drawn most freely are Rohlfs, Crescini, Appel and Grafström. I feel particularly indebted to Gerhard Rohlfs from whom I have drawn the basic orientation of my work. I wish to thank the Committee on University Scholarly Publications of the University of Colorado for its continued encouragement of my research and to express my gratitude for the generous grant accorded me. Finally, it is a pleasure to acknowledge my obligations to Charles Baker who volunteered his time and effort to draw up the word index.

FREDE JENSEN

April 1971. Boulder, Colorado

PHONETIC SYMBOLS AND DIACRITICAL SIGNS

[ ]	brackets are used for phonetic symbols
[wa]	Fr. *oi* in *noir*
[ö]	Fr. *eu, œu* in *neuf, cœur*
[u]	Fr. *ou* in *cour*
[y]	Fr. *u* in *mur*
[ə]	Fr. *e* in *me*
u̯	wau, semi-vowel
i̯	yod, semi-vowel
[jø]	Fr. *ieu* in *mieux*
[ð]	Engl. *th* in *them*
[j]	Engl. *y* in *yes*; the equivalent of i̯ and yod
[tš]	Engl. *ch* in *chief*
[dž]	Engl. *g* in *gentle*
[dz]	an affricate consisting of a *d* and a voiced *s*
[ts]	an affricate, voiceless counterpart of [dz]: *t* + voiceless *s*
[ź]	is used occasionally as the equivalent of [dz]
ẹ, ọ	close vowel sound
ę, ǫ	open vowel sound
ē	long vowel in Classical Latin (with any vowel)
ĕ	short vowel in Classical Latin (with any vowel)
c'r	indicates a secondary or Romance consonant cluster
cr	indicates a primary or Latin consonant cluster
>	becomes
<	comes from
*	indicates a hypothetical, non-attested form
' or `	used (outside of French words) to mark stress.

ABBREVIATIONS

acc.: accusative
Cat.: Catalan
CL: Classical Latin
fem.: feminine
Fr.: French
ind.: indicative
It.: Italian
Lat.: Latin
masc.: masculine
nom.: nominative
perf.: perfect
pers.: person
Pg.: Portuguese
plur.: plural
Pr.: Provençal
sing.: singular
Sp.: Spanish
subj.: subjunctive
VL: Vulgar Latin.

BIBLIOGRAPHICAL ABBREVIATIONS

Anglade: Anglade, J. *Grammaire de l'Ancien Provençal*. Paris: Klincksieck, 1921.
Appel: Appel, G. *Provenzalische Lautlehre*. Leipzig: Reisland, 1918.
Appel: *Chr.*: Appel, C. *Provenzalische Chrestomathie*, Leipzig: Reisland, 1930.
AR.: *Archivum Romanicum*, Genève - Firenze.
Badía Margarit: Badía Margarit, A. *Gramática histórica catalana*. Barcelona: Editorial Noguer, 1951.
Boutière: Boutière, J. and Schutz, A.-H. *Biographies des Troubadours*. Toulouse - Paris, 1950.
Brunel: Brunel, C. *Les plus anciennes chartes en langue provençale*. Paris: Picard, 1926, 1952.
Corominas: Corominas, J. *Diccionario crítico etimológico de la lengua castellana*. Madrid, 1954-1957.
Crescini: Crescini, V. *Manuale per l'avviamento agli studi provenzali*. Milano: Hoepli, 1926.
Elcock: Elcock, W. D. *The Romance Languages*. London: Faber and Faber, 1960.
FEW: Wartburg, W. von. *Französisches etymologisches Wörterbuch*. Bonn-Leipzig - Basel, 1922 ff.
Fouché: Fouché, P. *Phonétique historique du français*. Paris, 1953-1958.
Fouché: *Verbe*: Fouché, P. *Morphologie historique du français. Le Verbe*. Paris: Klincksieck, 1967.
Foulet: Foulet, L. *Petite Syntaxe de l'Ancien Français*. Paris: Champion, 1968.
Grafström: Grafström, Å. *Etude sur la Graphie des plus anciennes Chartes languedociennes*. Uppsala: Almqvist, 1958.
Grafström: *Morph.*: Grafström, Å. *Etude sur la Morphologie des plus anciennes Chartes languedociennes*. Uppsala: Almqvist, 1968.
Grandgent: Grandgent, C. H. *An Outline of the Phonology and Morphology of Old Provençal*. Boston: Heath, 1905.
Hamlin: Hamlin, F., Ricketts, P. T., and Hathaway, J. *Introduction à l'Etude de l'Ancien Provençal*. Genève: Droz, 1967.
Jeanroy: Jeanroy, A. *La Poésie lyrique des Troubadours*. Toulouse - Paris, 1934.

Lausberg: Lausberg, H. *Romanische Sprachwissenschaft*. Berlin: W. de Gruyter, 1958-1962.
Menéndez Pidal: Menéndez Pidal, R. *Manual de gramática histórica española*. Madrid: Espasa-Calpe, 1952.
Nyrop: Nyrop, Kr. *Grammaire historique de la Langue française*. Copenhagen: Gyldendal, 1924-1930.
REW: Meyer-Lübke, W. *Romanisches etymologisches Wörterbuch*. Heidelberg: Winter, 1935.
RF: *Romanische Forschungen*, Erlangen - Frankfurt.
Rheinfelder: Rheinfelder, H. *Altfranzösische Grammatik*. München: Max Hüber Verlag, 1963, 1967.
Riquer: Riquer, Martín de. *La lírica de los trovadores*. Barcelona, 1948.
RLR: *Revue des langues romanes*, Montpellier.
Rohlfs: Rohlfs, G. *Vom Vulgärlatein zum Altfranzösischen*. Tübingen: Niemeyer, 1960.
Rohlfs: *Hist. Gr.*: Rohlfs, G. *Historische Grammatik der italienischen Sprache*. Berne: Francke Verlag, 1954.
Schultz-Gora: Schultz-Gora, O. *Altprovenzalisches Elementarbuch*. Heidelberg: Winter, 1936.
Stimming: Stimming, A. *Bertran von Born*. Halle: Niemeyer, 1892.
Väänänen: Väänänen, V. *Introduction au Latin vulgaire*. Paris: Klincksieck, 1963.
Williams: Williams, E. B. *From Latin to Portuguese*. Philadelphia, 1962.
ZRPh: *Zeitschrift für romanische Philologie*, Halle.

THE PROVENÇAL LANGUAGE

Provençal is the written language which one encounters in Southern France from the 10th century, and which reaches its highest level of literary perfection in the troubadour poetry of the 12th - 13th centuries. [1]

The term *Provence* refers specifically to the regions located East of the Rhône river, but the wider use of the word *Provençal* as the language of Southern France is historically justified since it is derived from the name of the old Roman *Provincia Narbonensis*. The Provençal language shows a remarkable homogeneity with only negligible dialectal variations from one zone to the other; the poetic language thus takes the form of a *koiné* which is essentially based on the linguistic variety of the Limousin and Toulouse regions. Most of the great troubadour poets were natives of these areas, whereas Provence itself produced only very few famous writers. Hence, the term *Provençal* is misleading, however it *is* the most widely used appellation and the only one known to non-specialists.

The lack of any specific general term for the language of the troubadour poets is noteworthy. Quite frequently, it is referred to simply as *lenga romana,* when contrasted with Latin. [2] This is the term which François Raynouard tried to impose in the beginning

---

[1] Geographically, the language covers the entire area of Southern France with the exception of the old province of Aquitania where Gascon had developed as a separate language, in many ways different from Provençal, and often concurring, in various linguistic developments, with the languages of the Iberian Peninsula. See G. Rohlfs: *Le Gascon: Études de philologie pyrénéenne,* Halle, 1935.

[2] Appel (§ 1) quotes from Jaufré Rudel: *lo vers que chantam en plana lenga romana.* Guilhem de Peitieus offers his prayers *et en romans et en lati.*

of the 19th century, because he erroneously considered Provençal an intermediate step between Latin and the Romance languages which, viewed in this fashion, become neo-Provençal rather than neo-Latin.³

Limousin, which points to a precise dialectal zone, is linguistically a better term than *Provençal*. However, it was also used about Catalan from the 16th through the 19th century, and it probably owes its lack of success to the confusion resulting from this dichotomy. *Lenga d'oc*, based on the affirmative particle *oc* (< *hŏc*), seems to have been initially a geographical rather than a linguistic designation (cf. the old provincial name *Languedoc*). It led to the creation of the term *Occitania* from which the adjective *Occitan* was drawn, widely used by the Félibres and adopted by Jeanroy who, in 1945, published his *Histoire sommaire de la poésie occitane*. Another great French Provençalist, Joseph Anglade, adopted the term *Méridional*. This word reflects a somewhat restricted outlook, being suitable for Parisians only, whereas Italian or Spanish scholars would find it less felicitous. *Provençal* thus remains the most common and the most convenient term.

Provençal never acquired the status of a national language, nor did it ever designate the language of any single political state. It is a written language of the greatest cultural importance in medieval Europe as a vehicle for the oldest courtly poetry.

The Provençal language enjoyed a central position in Romania, bridging the gap between Gallo-Romance and Italo-Romance, between Gallo-Romance and Hispano-Romance, and thus, ultimately, between the Italic and the Iberian Peninsula.⁴ Its closest ties are with Catalan which, in its earliest stages, is considered by Rohlfs as "nichts anderes als eine regionale Abart des provenzalischen."⁵

---

³ A discussion of Raynouard's theory is found in Alberto Várvaro: *Linguistica Romanza*, Napoli, 1968, pps. 33-36.

⁴ "So ist das Provenzalische gleichsam ein Zentrum der Romania..... Es ist der sprachliche und kulturelle Knotenpunkt der Verbindung zwischen den beiden Halbinseln und andererseits zwischen ihnen und Nordfrankreich." (A. Kuhn: *Romanische Philologie*, vol. 1, Berne, 1951, p. 337). See also G. Rohlfs: *Einführung in das Studium der romanischen Philologie*, Heidelberg: Winter, 1966, p. 101.

⁵ Cf. Rohlfs, p. 53, note 101; consult also W. Meyer-Lübke: *Das Katalanische*, Heidelberg, 1925, pps. 1-4.

A BRIEF OUTLINE OF PROVENÇAL PHONOLOGY

The Vulgar Latin vocalic system is better preserved in Provençal than in French. Provençal keeps the free stressed *a* which French changes to an open *e*: *mare, tale, capra* > Pr. *mar, tal, cabra*; Fr. *mer, tel, chèvre*, and it keeps the *au* diphthong which, in French, is simplified to *o*: *auru, thesauru* > Pr. *aur, tezaur*; Fr. *or, trésor*. The close vowels *ę* (< *ē, ĭ, oe*) and *ǫ* (< *ō, ŭ*) are never diphthongized, while French breaks *ę* into *ei* > *oi* > [*wa*], and *ǫ* into *ou* > *eu* > [*ö*] if free and stressed: *tēla, habēre, valōre, hōra* > Pr. *tela, aver, valor, ora*; Fr. *toile, avoir, valeur, heure*. Provençal, like Portuguese, lacks the spontaneous dipththongization in a stressed free syllable of the open vowels *ĕ* and *ŏ*: *pĕde* > Pr. *pe*, Pg. *pé*, but Sp. *pié*, Fr. *pied*, It. *piede*; *rŏta* > Pr. Pg. *roda*, but Sp. *rueda*, It. *ruota*. But it has a conditioned diphthongization caused by a palatal or, at times, by a final -*u*; this development, however, is not obligatory: *dĕu* > *dieu, deu*; *nŏcte* > *nuoit, nueit* and also *noit*.[6] A relatively late feature is the palatalization of *ū* to [y] which

---

[6] This type of diphthongization exists also in French: *ĕxit* > *ieist > Old Fr. *ist*; *sĕx* > *sieis > *sis* > *six*; *nŏcte* > *nueit > *nuit*, where the palatal provokes a diphthongization in spite of the blocked position of the vowel. For Catalan, scholars cannot agree as to whether the change of *ĕ* to *i* and of *ŏ* to *u* in connection with a following palatal, stems from a simple inflexion or raising (cf. *a(u)scŭltat* > Sp. *escucha*, Pg. *escuta*), or whether it reflects the outcome of a conditioned diphthongization process (*ĕ* + yod > *iei > *i*, and *ŏ* + yod > *uei > *u, ui*). Badía Margarit (§§ 48, II and 51, II-III), after having weighed the pros and cons of the two theories, decides to straddle the fence : "nuestra exposición es compatible con las dos teorías mencionadas." Rohlfs (p. 55 note 103) adheres to the diphthongization theory: "Diese Diphthongierung gilt auch ... für das Katalanische und die Mundarten des spanischen Nordens."

Provençal shares with French: *mūru* > Pr. Fr. *mur*,[7] while Catalan retains *u*.[8]

In the realm of weak vowels, the most distinctive feature of Provençal is the very frequent retention of the penult in proparoxytones: *carcĕre* > *carcer*; *cassanu > *casse* or *casser*; *crescĕre* > *creisser*; *plangĕre* > *planher*; *vĭncĕre* > *venser*. Final *a* is kept as opposed to its weakening to [ə] in French: *pŏrta* > Pr. *porta*, Fr. *porte*.

Basic features of consonantal development are shared with French (and other languages of Western Romania): voicing in intervocalic position, unvoicing in final position, simplification of geminates.

Lenition of intervocalic voiceless stops reaches only the stage of voicing (*p, t, k* > *b, d, g*): *sapēre* > *saber*; *vīta* > *vida*; *amīca* > *amiga*, much the same as in Portuguese (*saber, vida, amiga*), whereas Spanish and French move on to the fricative level or develop further to complete elimination (quite frequent in French): Sp. *saber, vida, amiga* (with fricative pronunciation); Fr. *savoir, vie, amie*.

Other distinctive features of consonantal development in Provençal are the change of intervocalic *d* to a voiced *s*, mostly (though not always) spelled *z*: *vĭdēre* > *vezer*; *audīre* > *auzir*, the vocalization of final *v* to *u*: *nave* > *nau*; *clave* > *clau*, the development of intervocalic *tr* and *dr*, primary as well as secondary (original Latin clusters or obtained, in Vulgar Latin or common Romance, through the syncopation of a vowel), into yod + *r*: *pĕtra* > *peira*; *tropātor* > *trobaire*; *quadru* > *caire*; *crēdĕre* > *creire*, the retention

---

[7] As for the approximate date of this occurrence, cf. E. Richter, in *ZRPh*, vol. 41 p. 88 ff., and vol. 45, p. 385 ff. See also E. Richter: *Beiträge zur Geschichte der Romanismen*, Halle, 1934, p. 254 ff., and Fr. Schürr, in *RF*, vol. 50, p. 321. A detailed discussion is found in Fouché, vol. 2, p. 203 ff.

[8] Consult Badía Margarit (§ 53) for this important difference between Provençal and Catalan. Margarit favors the theory of a retention of [*u*] in Catalan, but other scholars consider [*u*] a regressive form, replacing an archaic Catalan [*y*]. This latter hypothesis, however, seems hardly plausible in view of the relatively late appearance of [*y*] in Gallo-Romance. A brief outline of some of the most important similarities and differences between Provençal and Catalan is furnished by B. E. Vidos: *Manual de lingüística románica*, Madrid: Aguilar, 1963, pps. 291-292.

(though far from general) of *k* and *g* before *a*: CL *caput* > VL *capu* > *cap*; *gallu* > *gal*; the development of a prosthetic vowel *e* with initial *s* + consonant: *schŏla* > *escola*; *spīna* > *espina*; *stare* > *estar*.

THE TROUBADOUR BIOGRAPHIES

A few excerpts from the troubadour biographies are given as samples of Provençal prose writings. These works, most of them by unknown authors, are mainly preserved in 13th and 14th century manuscripts and are written in a fairly simple and easy style. They consist of two different types of biographical compositions, known as *vidas* and *razós*, of which the former, usually rather limited in scope, contain precise information about the troubadour's life (date and place of birth, family, social position, travels, etc.), whereas the *razós* furnish an explanation of the poetic works themselves. *Vidas* and *razós* were probably the works of minstrels (*joglars*) who wanted to familiarize their audience with the authors as well as with the poems they were about to recite. The information contained in these prose works about the origin, life and love-affairs of the troubadour poets has been variously judged. Jeanroy is very negative in his assessment, and Boutière and Schutz consider them a strange mixture of truth and fiction, with fiction far outweighing truth. Strónski and Martín de Riquer treat them more fairly, giving credence to the concise factual information of the *vidas*, but relegating to the realm of fancy most of the amorous adventures described in the *razós*. [9]

---

[9] Cf. Jeanroy, vol. 1, p. 132; A. Jeanroy: "Les Biographies des Troubadours," in *AR*, vol. 1, 1917, p. 289; S. Strónski: *Le Troubadour Folquet de Marseille*, Krakow, 1910; Riquer, pps. X-XIII; and a fairly recent critical edition of the biographies by J. Boutière and A.-H. Schutz: *Biographies des Troubadours*, Paris - Toulouse, 1950, pps. XI-XVII.

The prose samples are drawn from the *vidas* of Bertran de Born and Peire Vidal, and they also comprise a *razó* which sets forth in detail the political and historical events that form the subject matter of a *sirventes* by Bertran de Born: *Pois lo gens terminis floris.*

1. BERTRAN DE BORN

Bertrans de Born si fo us chastelas de l'eveschat de Peiregorc, senher d'un chastel que avia nom Autafort. Totz temps ac guerra ab totz los sieus vezis: ab lo comte de Peiregorc et ab lo vescomte de Lemotges et ab so fraire Constanti et ab Richart, tan quan fo coms de Peitau. Bos chavaliers fo e bos guerriers e bos domneiaire e bos trobaire e savis e be parlans e saup tractar mals e bes, et era senher totas vetz quan si volia de.l rei Henric d'Englaterra e de.l filh de lui. Mas totz temps volia qu'ilh aguessen guerra ensems, lo paire e.l filhs e.lh fraire, l'us ab l'autre, et totz temps volc que.l reis de Franza e.l reis d'Englaterra aguessen guerra ensems. E s'ilh avian patz ni tregua, ades si penava e.s perchassava ab sos sirventes de desfar la patz e de mostrar com chascus era desonratz en la patz.

Bertrans de Born si fo us chastelas de l'eveschat de Peiregorc
'Bertran de Born was a nobleman from the diocese of Périgord.'

The name *Bertrans* appears in the nominative case with a flexional *-s*. Old Provençal, like Old French, has a two-case system in the masculine declension, based on the retention of final Latin *s* or the addition of a final *s* through analogy. An example of the masculine declension in *-us* will serve as an illustration of this flexion:

    nom sing. *murus* > *murs*   nom. plur. *muri* > *mur*
    acc. sing. *murum* > *mur*   acc. plur. *muros* > *murs*.

Born is a small township in the commune of Salagnac (Dordogne).

The adverbial *si* here has the conjunctional function of connecting the verb with the preceding subject. Its widespread use with proper nouns in Provençal is well attested in the *vidas*, from where examples are easily gathered: *lo coms de Peitieus si fo uns dels majors cortes del mon*; *Cercamons si fo uns joglars de Gascoingna*; *Girautz de Borneill si fo de Limozi*. The adverbial *si* is extremely common in Old French as well; its main functions are to coordinate two clauses, in which case it is more or less the equivalent of *et*, or to introduce the main clause, following a preceding subordinate clause: *Lors li mostrent une chanbrete, si dient: "Leanz l'encloez"* (Chrétien de Troyes, *Yvain*, v. 5560-61); *Quant la chanbre fu desfermee, si se leva et oï messe* (ib., v. 4024-25). An adverbial *si* is also encountered in Old Italian. [10]

---

[10] For the various uses of adverbial *si* in Old French, cf. Foulet, §§ 439-442; for the use of *si* in Old Italian, especially in Northern Italian dialects, cf. Rohlfs: Hist. Gr., § 760.

fo < *fŭit*. *O* is the regular outcome of Latin *ŭ*, and the 3. pers. sing. ending -*it* is lost very early in Provençal. Through a process of *umlaut* or metaphony, Provençal changes *o* to *u* [y] in the 1. and 2. pers. sing. under the influence of -*ī*: *fŭī* > *fui*; *fŭ(i)stī* > *fust*. The other forms of this perfect (*fo, fom, fǫtz, foron*), lacking an -*ī* ending in Latin, are unaffected by the *umlaut* feature, whereas French generalizes the [y] from *fui* < *fŭī* throughout the entire perfect. Italian has kept *o* only in the 2. pers. sing. and plur. (*fosti, foste* as opposed to *fui, fu, fummo, furono*), but *fusti, fuste* and *foro* are all attested in Old Italian along with other dialectal variants. [11] The pronunciation of *ǫ* (< *ŭ, ō*) was at times closed all the way down to *u*. Appel mentions this pronunciation, but with some reservation, since the graph *u* mostly appears for CL *ŭ*: *mult* < *mŭltu*; *ultra* < *ŭltra*, etc. [12]

us < *ūnus*. Final *n* is either kept or dropped in Provençal, and *n* is likewise unstable before flexional *s*: *bĕne* > *ben, be*; *manu* > *man, ma*; *ūnus* > *uns, us*. This instability of final *n* is proof of a lesser degree of nasalization in Southern France than in the North.

chastelas < *castellanus*. Provençal usually keeps *k* intact before *a*, but the palatalization to [tš], spelled *ch*, is widespread, especially in the regions bordering on the French linguistic domain, and also in Limousin, which accounts for its frequency in troubadour poetry. [13]

eveschat is derived from *epǐscopu* combined with the suffix -*ātu*. *Evesque* is a French borrowing which replaces the Provençal form *bisbe* or *bispe*, but the treatment of the suffix is indigenous: -*ātu* > -*at* as opposed to Fr. -*é* (cf. Fr. *évêché*). [14]

Peiregorc: le Périgord (Dordogne).

---

[11] Cf. Rohlfs: Hist. Gr., § 583.
[12] Cf. Appel, § 29; and Grandgent, § 33.
[13] For the geographical distribution of *ca*- versus *cha*-, cf. Crescini, pps. 21-22; and Anglade, pps. 161-162. See also P. Meyer, in *Romania*, vol. 24, p. 529, and vol. 30, pps. 393-398.
[14] For French elements in Provençal, see Appel, § 15. A postulated * *epīscopu* (or learned treatment of *ĭ*) would account for the *i* of *bisbe*. The loss of initial *e* may also affect the French borrowing, giving Pr. *vesque*; cf. It. *vescovo*.

senher d'un chastel que avia nom Autafort 'lord of a castle which was called Hautefort.'

senher < *sĕnior*. This is a nom. sing. used in apposition with the subject *Bertrans*. N + yod gives a palatalized *n* for which Provençal often uses the graph *nh* (cf. *lh* as a graph for palatalized *l*).[15] The supporting vowel *e* is inserted before *r*, if the preceding consonant is a palatal: *mĕlior* > *melher*; *pĕior* > *peier*. *Sĕnior, sĕniŏrem* is an example of the imparisyllabic flexion, characterized by a different number of syllables in the two cases of the singular, and, more importantly, by a shift in stress: *sĕnior* > *sénher*; *sĕniŏre* > *senhór*, Fr. *seigneur*. The French nominative *sire* is derived from **sĕior*, a weak form which arose through its use as a title.

que. Provençal uses either *qui* or *que* in the nominative; *que* may originally have come from neuter *quod* or *quĭd*, replacing masc. *qui* and fem. *quae*.

avia < *habēbat*. The imperfect ending *-ēbat* gives *-ea*, then *-ia*. In verbs like *habēbat* and *debēbat*, the second *b* is lost by dissimilation, and the ending thus obtained is then generalized from these cases. The change of *-ea* to *-ia* reflects a strong trend in Romance towards a raising of *e* to *i* in hiatus (cf. *vĭa* > Pr. It. Pg. *via*, Sp. *vía*, but Fr. *voie*). Rohlfs and Crescini derive *-ia* from an archaic and popular ending *-ībam* which replaces CL *-iebam* and spreads to the other conjugations (with the exception of the *-are* group), but other scholars seem to adopt the theory of a raising in hiatus.[16]

avia nom < *habēbat nōmen*. The same construction is found in Old French: *Marie ai nun, si sui de France* (Marie de France, *Fables*, épilogue 4). *Aver nom* 'to be called' is usually followed by a nominative case: *avia nom Artusetz* (STIMMING, 13, 20-21); *avia nom Johans ses Terra* (ib., III, 2, p. 141), but not exclusively so

---

[15] Portuguese borrowed these graphs from Provençal. For a discussion of this problem, see Williams, § 27, 6.

[16] Cf. Lausberg, §§ 187, 873; Crescini, p. 115; and Rohlfs, p. 66. For the change to *-ia* in Portuguese and Spanish, see Williams, § 164; and Menéndez Pidal, § 11,2, neither of whom mentions *-ībam*.

as shown by the following examples with the accusative: *avia nom Cercamon* (HAMLIN, 7, 3); *ac nom Marcabrun* (ib., 7, 4).

Totz temps ac guerra ab totz los sieus vezis: 'he waged war continuously against all his neighbors.'

totz does not go back to CL *tōtos,* but reflects a VL *tŏttos,* condemned by Consentius as barbaric. It is uncertain whether this goes back to a reinforcement with *tot* or to a simple repetition * *tottotus* for the sake of expressivity.[17]

temps < *tĕmpus.* P is a Latinizing graph without phonetic value. A similar non-etymological *p* is sometimes found in the old Provençal deeds: *veszcomps, veszcompte,* from Lat. *cŏmes, cŏmĭte.*

ac < *habuit.* The *u* of perfect forms in *-ui* was regularly changed into a sound that must have been very similar to the Germanic [w], since it underwent the same changes as this latter sound: [w] > [gw] > [g]. An auxiliary sound [g] is added, and [w] itself is then dropped; the spelling *gu* is normally used before a front vowel, but appears also elsewhere as a mere graph for [g]. Inside a word, the cluster *g* + *u̯* did exist in Latin in words like *lĭngua,* and this may help explain the addition of the auxiliary sound [g]. The *-ui* perfects develop as follows: *tenuistī* > * *tenwist* > *tenguist,* and, with unvoicing of *g* to *k* in final position: *tenuit* > * *tenwet* > * *tengwet* > *tenc*; *habuit* > *ac* (with loss of *b* before *u̯* as compared with the retention of the liquid *n* in *tenc*). The 3. pers. sing. ending *-it* is lost early: *fŭit* > *fo*; *valet* > *val.*

guerra, from Germanic .* *werra,* is an example of the above-mentioned treatment of initial Germanic *w-*. The stage [gw] is kept in Italian, whereas Gallo-Romance and Hispano-Romance have simplified [gw] to [g].

---

[17] Cf. Rohlfs, p. 77. Lausberg (§§ 491, 494) lists *tŏttus* with variants like *glūtus - glŭttus* which observe the sequence of long vowel + single consonant or short vowel + long consonant. *Tŏttus* would then, like *stēlla,* represent an early violation of this sequence rule.

ab < *apu(d)*. The final *d* was lost already in Vulgar Latin times, but the subsequent development of VL *apu* to *ab* is not regular. A *p* which becomes final is normally kept in Provençal: *lŭpu* > *lop*; CL *caput* > VL *capu* > *cap*, whereas intervocalic *p* is voiced to *b*: *lŭpa* > *loba*; *sapēre* > *saber*. Since a voicing cannot normally occur at the end of a word, we have to turn to syntactic phonetics for an explanation of *ab*. The word *apud* is proclitic in nature, which means that, together with the word or words it governs, it forms only one phonetic unit (*mot phonétique*); when appearing before a word beginning with a vowel, *p* is therefore intervocalic and can voice, and it is this form which is generalized. The proclitic nature of the word is also evident in the strong trend towards an assimilation of *b* with the following consonant, yielding variants like *ap, am, an* and even *amb*, probably a combination of *ab + am*: *am lor* 'with them'; *amb una oz am doas tornadas* 'with one or two refrains.' [18]

los sieus is the strong form of the possessive in the 3. pers. plur.; the article is used with the strong forms, not with the weak: *lo mieus amics*, but *mos amics*. Morphologically, the nom. sing. *sieus* does not come from *sŭus*, but from ** sĕus*, obtained by analogy with *mĕus*. The diphthongization of *ĕ* before *-u* being optional, *mĕus* is continued either as *meus* or *mieus*; likewise we get: *tŭus* > ** tĕus* > *teus, tieus*, and *sŭus* > ** sĕus* > *seus, sieus*. The form we have here is, of course, the acc. plur. (<* *sĕos* < *sŭos*). In direct contact with a stressed open *e*, final *u* loses its syllabic value, but is kept as the second part of a diphthong: *mĕu* > *meu*; *dĕu* > *deu*; *iūdaeu* > *juzeu*. This appears to be a somewhat more general phenomenon in Provençal than in French where it occurs in a couple of learned words: *dĕu* > *Dieu*; *Mathĕu* > *Mathieu*, but does not affect the possessives. The *ieu* combination is resolved into [jø] in modern French.

---

[18] For the use of *apud* instead of CL *cum*, see Rohlfs, pps. 62-63, note 121; for the preposition *ab* in the deeds, see Grafström, § 76, 2, c. A continuation of CL *cum* 'with' is not uncommon in Provençal: *e fez cansos com avinens sons* (Boutière, p. 256, 2-3); *com bels ditz e com bels honramenz e com bellas promissions* (ib., p. 193, 8-9).

vezis does not come from CL *vīcīnos*, but from a dissimilated form in Vulgar Latin, *vēcīnos*; compare Sp. *vecinos* and Fr. *voisins*. Similar cases of vowel dissimilation are: *fīnīre* > *fenir*; *dīvīnāre* > *devinar*.

ab lo comte de Peiregorc et ab lo vescomte de Lemotges et ab so fraire Constanti 'against the count of Périgord and against the viscount of Limoges and againt his own brother Constantin'.

comte < *cŏmĭte* is the acc. sing. form; the nom. sing. is *coms* < *cŏmes* (cf. Old Fr. *cuens*). *Cŏmes - cŏmĭte* is an imparisyllabic noun which does not show any shift in stress (compare also *hŏmo - hŏmĭne*). *Vescomte* shows popular treatment of the prefix, whereas forms in *vi-* and *vice-*, such as Fr. *vicomte, vidame, vice-consul,* are learned. There are signs that *coms* could join the *murs - mur* declension in Provençal through the creation of an acc. *vescont*, drawn by analogy from the nom. *vescoms*, as in this example, from Boutière, p. 58, 5-6: *e comenset ades a gerejar N'Aseimar, lo vescont de Lemotges*; compare also: *a coms, marques, a baros d'aut afar* (Crescini, p. 253,85), where *coms* appears as an acc. plur.

Lemotges continues the name of a Celtic tribe, the *Lemovicos*. Anglade explains the phonological development through a change of the rare cluster *v'c* into *d'c*: *Lemovicos* > * *Lemodicos* > *Lemotjes*. [19]

so < *sŭum* represents the weak form of the possessive: CL *sŭum* > VL * *som* > *son, so* with an unstable *n*. The retention of final *m* in Vulgar Latin is normal for monosyllables; cf *rĕm* > *ren, re*; Fr. *rien*; *quĕm* > Sp. *quién*.

fraire < *fratre*. In Provençal, both *tr* and *dr* give yod + *r*; the *ai* diphthong represents a combination of *a* with this yod, and is not the result of any vocalic diphthongization process. Other examples of this development: *pĕtra* > *peira*; *latro* > *laire*. [20]

---

[19] Cf. Anglade, p. 148.
[20] Crescini (pps. 42-43) gives a physiological explanation of this change, according to which *t* and *d* go via a fricative [ð] to *į*. He points out that

et ab Richart, tan quan fo coms de Peitau 'and against Richard, as long as he was count of Poitou'.

Richart < Germanic *Rikhard*. The palatalization of *k* before *a* is a relatively late phenomenon which also affects words borrowed from Germanic; cf. *Carolus* > Fr. *Charles*. This is Richard Coeur-de-Lion, King of England and Count of Poitou from 1169 to 1189.

tan < *tantu*. Final *nt* and *nd* are reduced to a stable *n*; other examples of this development: *mŭndu* > *mon*; *monte* > *mon*; *quando* > *can*; *quantu* > *can*.

quan < *quantu*. Before *a*, [kw] was reduced early to [k]; *quan* and *can* are thus mere graphical variants, similarly *quar* and *car* < *quare*. This graphical alternance even led to erroneous spellings like *quaitiu* < *captīvu*, where no *qu* was etymologically involved. [21]

Peitau < *Pĭctavu*. *V* is lost before a back vowel, and the resulting *au* diphthong is kept in Provençal. Several Vulgar Latin examples of the loss of *v* in this position are encountered in the *Appendix Probi*: *rivus non rius*; *pavor non paor*; *flavus non flaus*. It is a common feature of French: *pavōre* > *paour* > *peur*; *pavōne* > *paon*. [22]

Bos chavaliers fo e bos guerriers 'he was a brave knight and a brave warrior'.

bos chavaliers, bos guerriers are in the nom. sing., used as predicates of *fo*. The use of the perfect tense in a purely descriptive connotation corresponds to Old French usage. In most cases, it is the perfect which encroaches upon what, from the point of view of modern French, is the domain of the imperfect. Thus, we find the

---

the same change occurs as a dialectal feature of Danish, notably in some dialects of Jutland: *Petru* > *Pedr* > *Peðr* > *Pejr*; cf. Pr. *Peire*.

[21] Grandgent (§ 62,2) seems to believe that [kw] was maintained in pronunciation in the Western portions of the "Midi."

[22] Cf. Appel, § 42a; and Lausberg, § 374. For the Vulgar Latin examples, see Elcock, p. 31; and Väänänen, § 90.

perfect used in introductory enunciations which furnish the background for actions about to be narrated, and it may even serve to describe lasting qualities, to indicate a person's profession etc., as a few examples will show: *Girautz de Salaingnac si fo de Caersin, del castel de Salaignac. Joglars fo; ben adregz hom fo e ben cortes* (Boutière, p. 201, 1-3); (*Sordels*) *fo avinens hom de la persona, e fo bons chantaire e bons trobaire, e grans amaires; mas mout fo truans e fals vas dompnas* (ib., p. 322, 2-4); (*Raymun Jorda*) *fon avinens e larcs e bos d'armas, e saup trobar e ben entendre* (ib., p. 280, 2-3). But other examples are available of exactly the same sentence structures in which the imperfect is used: (*Ponz de Capduoill*) *sabia ben trobar e violar e cantar* (ib., p. 257,3); (*Elias Cairels*) *era laboraire d'aur e d'argent* (ib., p. 93,2); *lo coms de Rodes si era mout adreics e mout valens, e si era trobaire* (ib., p. 82, 1-2). These few examples clearly show that the lack of any definite rules governing tense use, so characteristic of Old French syntax, can also be observed in Provençal, and this is very strikingly illustrated in our excerpt by the alternance between *mas totz temps volia* and *et totz temps volc*.

chavaliers < *caballarius*. The palatization of *k* before *a*, which occurs in some regions of the South, does not affect pretonic free *a*, as it does in French where *a*, in this particular position, is palatalized to [ə]: *chevaliers*.

guerriers. The development of the *-ariu* suffix in Gallo-Romance is obscure and rather complex. The oldest form in Provençal seems to have been *-er*: *cavaler, primer*, but *-ier* is more common, and forms in *-eir, -ir* are also encountered: *cavaler, cavalier, cavaleir*. Numerous explanations have been offered to solve the problems which the development of *-ariu* poses for French and Provençal. Nyrop and Grandgent postulate a change of *-ariu* to *-ĕriu*, attested in the *Glossary of Reichenau*; Thomas, Anglade and, more recently, Rheinfelder propose an influence of the Germanic suffix *-(h)ari* (> * *-eri*, with *e* arising from a metaphony caused by *-ī*). While Grandgent finds this theory "promising", Appel, on the other hand, does not accept it for Provençal where *-ier*, in his view, is a borrowing from French. Rohlfs also expresses doubts, or at least reservations, concerning any Germanic (Frankish) influence on the

-*ariu* suffix, theories which he finds "wenig wahrscheinlich, auf alle Fälle nicht endgültig bewiesen." [23]

e bos domneiaire e bos trobaire e savis e be parlans 'attentive to women and an excellent poet, intelligent and very eloquent'.

The noun *domneiaire* is drawn from the verb *domnejar* 'to court a lady', based on *domina* and *-idiare*, a verbal suffix of Greek origin. The noun is formed from the verb by means of the *-ator* suffix, and it appears here in the nom. sing. It is not easily determined whether the intervocalic *i* (or *j*) was pronounced [j] or [dž]. Grandgent and Crescini both suggest a geographical distribution of these two sounds, Grandgent giving preference to [dž], while Crescini observes that troubadour poets seem to favor [j] in rhymes, and he concludes philosophically: "Rimane però l'incertezza." [24]

trobaire < *tropātor* is the nom. case (cf. Fr. *trouvère*); the acc. is *trobador* < *tropatōre*. The *trobador* is the poet who writes the literary work, and who also composes the accompanying music, as opposed to the *joglar* (Fr. *jongleur*) who recites the poem to the public. The verb * *tropare* (> *trobar*, Fr. *trouver*) is usually derived from the Greek rhetorical term *tropos*; strange and not sufficiently explained is the semantic change from 'compose a literary work' to the very general meaning 'to find'. [25] In *tropātor* > *trobaire*, the *t'r* cluster gives yod + *r* with *e* as a supporting vowel; *tropatōre* > *trobador*, on the other hand, shows the regular development of intervocalic *t* to *d*. Other examples of this imparisyllabic flexion are: *cantātor* > *cantaire*; *cantatōre* > *cantador*; *ĭmperātor* > *emperaire*; *ĭmperatōre* > *emperador*.

savis is derived from * *sapius* via * *sabius*. In learned words, the *i* may remain syllabic instead of becoming a yod and palatalizing the preceding consonant: *fluviu* > *fluvi*; *oliu* > *oli*; this as opposed to the popular development of *b* + yod to [dž]: *rŭbeu* >

---

[23] See Rohlfs, p. 116 note 283, for an admirable presentation of the problem. References are numerous: Appel, § 33c; Grandgent, § 23, 1, V; Crescini, p. 5; Rheinfelder, § 275; Fouché, vol. 2, p. 413. For Italian, see Rohlfs: Hist. Gr., § 1113.
[24] Cf. Grandgent, § 65, 6, 2; and Crescini, pps. 35-36.
[25] Cf. Rohlfs, p. 72, and note 155.

rog(e), which would have given * *sag(e)*. It is necessary to postulate an early voicing in intervocalic position of *p* to *b*: * *sapiu* > * *sabiu*, in order to obtain the form *savi*, since intervocalic *p* gives *b* (*sapēre* > *saber*), while intervocalic *b* goes to *v* (*faba* > *fava*; *caballu* > *caval*). The same change is required for Fr. *sage*, since *p* + yod normally gives a voiceless result in French (*sapiam* > *sache*).[26]

e saup tractar mals e bes 'and he knew how to handle good and evil'.

saup < *sapuit*. Perfects in -*ui* with a stem ending in *p* did not undergo the usual change to *g, c* (cf. *tenuistī* > *tenguist*; *tenuit* > *tenc*); instead, *p* was left intact, and *u* was released in front. The reason for this important exception to the rule is not clear.[27]

tractar < *tractare*. Provençal shows two collateral developments of the *ct* cluster: a palatal [tš] or yod + *t*, spelled *ch* and *it* respectively, whether the cluster occurs in a final position or inside a word: *factu* > *fach, fait*; *fractūra* > *frachura, fraitura*. *Tractar* must be a learned form or a case of learned spelling.[28]

et era senher totas vetz quan si volia de.l rei Henric d'Englaterra e de.l filh de lui 'and whenever he wanted, he was able to dominate King Henry of England and the king's son'.

era is a continuation of the Classical Latin imperfect *ĕrat*; cf. Old Fr. *er(e)t, ier(e)t*. Since all other imperfects have an -*ava* or -*ia* ending (cf. *cantābam* > *cantava*; *credē(b)am* > *crezia*), this complete isolation in the paradigm makes *era* vulnerable to morpho-

---

[26] For the French development of * *sabiu* > *sage*, see Rheinfelder, § 532; and compare Sp. *pichón* with Fr. *pigeon* < * *pīpiōne*. For * *sapius*, created as some sort of a compromise between *sapiens* and *sapidus*, see Rohlfs, p. 71.
[27] For a detailed discussion of these two perfect types, *ac* versus *saup*, from *habuit* and *sapuit*, see Grafström: Morph., § 65, b. For the identical development of *pu* to *up* in Spanish (*sapui* > * *saupe* > *sope* > *supe*, with *u* obtained from an analogy with *pude*), cf. Menéndez Pidal, § 120, 3; and for Portuguese, where *au* gives *ou* (*habuit* > * *haubet* > *houve*; *sapuit* > *soube*), cf. Williams, §§ 167, 3; 186, 5 and 196, 7.
[28] The geographical distribution of [tš] and *it* in Provençal is shown by Crescini (pps. 27-28). It is interesting to note how Provençal here bridges the gap between the Spanish and the French evolution of *ct*: *lacte* > Sp. *leche*, Fr. *lait*; *factu* > Sp. *hecho*, Fr. *fait*. The development to *it* is the norm in Portuguese: *lacte* > *leite*; *factu* > *feito*.

logical pressure leading to the creation of *eravám*, *eravátz* for *erám* and *erátz* (< *ĕrāmus*, *ĕrātis*). These are, however, rare forms; they occur, for instance, in the novel *Jaufre*: *tuit eravam marrit*. In Old French, the isolated position of *ere*, *iere* (< *ĕram*) makes it incapable of resisting the encroachments of an analogical *esteie*, which completely replaces *ere* after 1300.

vetz < *vĭce*. A prepalatal final *k* (from -*ce* or -*ci*) gives *tz* in Provençal: *vōce* > *votz*, whereas French has an additional release of yod: *vōce* > *voiz* > *voix*. In the above sentence, *vetz* appears as a plural, but is left unchanged, as is most often the case with nouns ending in *s* or *tz*; cf. *cen vetz* 'a hundred times'. The addition of a syllable -*es* in the plural is very rare in Old Provençal lyrical poetry, but occurs not infrequently in the old deeds as well as in some post-classical texts: *de totz los mases* 'of all the farm houses' (Brunel, 16,8); *donam nostres corses e nostras animas a Dieu* 'we give our body and soul to God' (ib., 108,2); *per lor meteisses* 'by themselves' (ib., 315,10); *e mot geta diverses frugz* 'and it yields different varieties of fruit' (from the *Breviari d'Amor*, Appel: Chr., 115, 157). Anglade points to cases of -*es* in some of the modern dialects: *pas* - *passes*; *mes* - *meses*, etc. The deeds contain rare examples of the extended form used in the nom. sing. of the -*us* declension; *lo quals mases* (Brunel, 412,5).

si volia < *sē* + *volē(b)at*. Intransitive verbs are often used reflexively; the form of the reflexive pronoun is either *se* or *si*.

Henric d'Englaterra: Henry II Plantagenet, King of England from 1154 to 1189.

de.l < *de* + *ĭllu* is an example of an enclitic construction, quite frequent in the older stages of Gallo-Romance. Weak pronouns, articles, etc. are often used enclitically, supported by the preceding word with which they form one single phonetic emission. This usage was common in Old French (cf. *jol* = *jeo le*; *ses* = *se les*), but after the *Saint Alexis*, preference was given to the modern proclitic construction with weak words supported by the following verb.

de.l filh de lui. This construction is not uncommon; it serves as a clear indication of possession, where the normal phrase (here *del sieu filh*) might be misinterpreted (it could refer to Bertran's own son). It is frequently found in Old French; cf. *et estoit la char de li perse, seche et megre* (G. de Saint Pathus, *les Miracles de Saint Louis*, X, 14).

Mas totz temps volia qu'ilh aguessen guerra ensems 'but he always wanted them to wage war against one another'.

mas is probably a weakened form of *mais* < * *majis* < *magis*. Diphthongs may often lose the yod element in Provençal: *cuida* > *cuda*; *tuit* > *tut*; *vair* > *var*, etc.[29]

ilh < *ĭllī*. The nom. plur. of the masc. personal pronoun in the 3. pers. is *il* or *ilh*; the corresponding sing. form is *el* or *elh*. The phonetic development of *el* (< *ĭlle*) and *il* (< *ĭllī*) is regular, whereas French shows the *umlaut* feature, caused by *-ī*, also in the sing. for which one must postulate a change from *ĭlle* to * *ĭllī* (> Fr. *il*). Graphs in *-lh* or *-ll* indicate a palatalization which could occur whenever the pronoun appeared before a vowel. It is quite possible that even the graph *-l* itself may stand for a palatalized *l* at times as evident in the following words, quoted from the old deeds: *melor* (< *mĕliōre*), *moler* (< *mŭliĕre*), *cosel* (< *consĭliu*).[30]

aguessen < *habuissent*. Provençal, like French, draws its imperfect subjunctive from the Latin pluperfect subjunctive. The phonetic development recalls the regular treatment of the *ui* perfects where a *g* or *c* is obtained from the *u̯* (cf. *habuit* > *ac*); the two forms are built on the same stem.

ensems. The etymology is *insĭmul*.[31] Final *l* is dropped in polysyllabic words.[32] *N* usually drops before *s* in Vulgar Latin: CL

---

[29] Cf. Appel, § 34; Crescini, p. 35; and Rohlfs, p. 76. A proclitic form *mas* is attested already in Vulgar Latin, giving Pr. Old Cat. Sp. *mas*. See Badía Margarit, § 47, II, B; and also Menéndez Pidal (§ 128, 1) who mentions the existence of a proclitic *mas* in the *Glosas Emilianenses*.

[30] See the chapter, "Notations de 1 mouillé," in Grafström (§ 74). For Italian *egli*, replacing a phonological *elli*, see Rohlfs: Hist. Gr., § 436.

[31] See REW 4465 *insĭmul*. The other etymologies mentioned by Meyer-Lübke: * *ĭn-sĕmul* and *in + sĕmel*, are prompted by various deviations in Romance; It. *insieme* and Old Sp. *ensiemo* owe their diphthong to a short *e*, and *sĕmel* would account for the final vowel in Italian.

[32] Cf. Appel (§ 51) who points out that words like *Gabriel* and *Micael* are of a learned nature. Provençal also has the form *ensemble* where a *b* is inserted into the *m'l* cluster, and a supporting vowel is added.

mensa > VL *mesa*, even in combinations with a prefix like *in-* or *con-*. Following a prefix, Provençal has both forms, with or without *n*; where *n* is lost, the spelling *ss* is often used to indicate the voiceless quality of the consonant: *ensems* and *essems*, *conselh* and *cosselh*, *ensenhar* and *essenhar*. The preservation of *n* stems from morphological pressure from words where the prefixes appeared before consonants other than *s*, *v* and *f*, as well as from the compound nature of the words in question. The *s* that is added at the end, is a so-called adverbial *s*, drawn by analogy from the many Latin adverbs ending in *-s*: *prius*, *mĕlius*, *pĕius*, etc. It came to be considered, in Provençal as well as in Old French, as a characteristic morphological feature of adverbs (cf. Old Fr. *ores*, *onques*, etc.).

lo paire e.l filhs el.lh fraire, l'us ab l'autre 'the father and the son and the brothers, one against the other'.

lo. The definite article in the masc. sing., nom. and acc., is *lo*; in the plural, we find *li* in the nom., *los* in the acc. The enclitic form of *lo* is *.l*, while the plur. form *li* gives *.lh* enclitically. *E.lh fraire* would therefore have to be a plur. form (*frater* and *fratri* both give *fraire*), although other manuscripts have *.l*. The reference found in note 30 should be consulted for the interpretation of these graphs. The elided form of the article is *l'*.

filhs < *fīlius*. Palatal *l* is kept in Provençal even before a consonant, as opposed to French where it is vocalized or lost: * *trapalios* > *travauz* > *travaux*; *fīlius* > *fitz* > *fils* (with a purely graphical *l*).

e totz temps volc que.l reis de Franza e.l reis d'Englaterra aguessen guerra ensems 'and he always wanted the King of France and the King of England to wage war against one another'.

volc < *voluit*. Perfects in *ui* drop the preceding consonant, if it is a labial or a dental: *dēbuit* > *dec*; *habuit* > *ac*; *pŏtuit* > *poc*; but the liquids *l*, *n* and *r* are kept in this position: *valuit* > *valc*; *dŏluit* > *dolc*; *meruit* > *merc*; *vēnit* > * *venuit* > *venc*.

Franza < * *Frankia*. The *ki̯* cluster is palatalized to *ti̯*, then assibilated to *ts* which is reduced to *s* before or during the literary period. This very early reduction to s accounts for the hesitation in graph between z [ts] and s: *Franza - Fransa*; *Proenza - Proensa* (< *Provĭncia*); *forsa - forza* (< * *fŏrtia*).

E s'ilh avian patz ni tregua, ades si penava e.s perchassava ab sos sirventes 'And if they were at peace or had established a truce, he would immediately make an effort with his *sirventes*'.

ni, as seen from this example, does not always carry a negative meaning. The etymology is *nĕc* which gives *ne*; the change to *ni* may have originated from its use before a vowel: *ne amic* > *ni amic*.

tregua comes from Gothic * *triggwa* which also is continued in It. Sp. *tregua*. Coexisting with *tregua* in Provençal is *treva*, a continuation of Frankish * *triuwa* which also yields Old Fr. *trive* and Fr. *trêve*.

The origin of the adverb *adęs* cannot be *ad ĭpsu*, since intervocalic *d* gives a voiced *s* (cf. *vĭdere* > *vezer*), and since short *ĭ* would give a close *e*. The solution most commonly offered is a combination of *ad id ĭpsu* > * *addĭpsu*, where *dd* is simplified to *d*. The open *ę* comes from an analogy with *ad prĕssu* > *apręs*.

penava. The imperfect ending of the *-are* conjugation represents the normal phonetic outcome of *-ābat*, whereas *b* is dropped in the other conjugations. Compare also the Old French dialectal form *chanteve* < *cantabat*.

perchassava. * *Captiare* > *casar* or *cassar*, graphical variants which both represent a voiceless *s* coming from the assibilation of *tị* to *ts* with a subsequent early reduction of *ts* to *s* (cf. *Franza* above). *P* is lost when preceding a *tị* cluster; compare the retention of the liquid *n* in *Franza*. The prefix *per-* is used for reinforcement; cf. Lat. *factum* and *perfectum*. An example from the *Glossary of Reichenau* can perhaps best illustrate this use of *per*: *pergrandem* : *valde grandum*.

sirventes. This poetic genre was much favored by the troubadour poets; its content was mostly satirical or political. Etymologically, *sirventes* may be related to *sirvens* 'servant,' since it was normally composed by a member of the household of a king or a powerful lord for the purpose of defending him or attacking his enemies.[33]

de desfar la patz e de mostrar com chascus era desonratz en la patz 'to break the peace and to show how everyone was dishonored when living in peace.'

desfar. Provençal has both *faire* and *far*. While *faire* represents the regular outcome of *facĕre* after an early loss of the unstressed *e*,[34] *far* goes back to a popular infinitive *fare*, which was probably created under the influence of *dare* and *stare* (cf. It. *fare*).

mostrar < *monstrare*. The loss of *n* before *s* reflects an early Vulgar Latin change; Fr. *montrer* is learned.

com < VL *quomo* < CL *quomodo*. To VL *quomo* were often added various particles: Provençal has the form *coma* from a combination of *quomo* and *ad* or *ac*; and *quomo* + *et* gives Fr. *comme* and It. *come*.

chascus shows an early influence of Greek *kata* on Latin *quisque unus*, as is the case also of Old Fr. *chascun* > Fr. *chacun*. Sp. *cada uno* continues Greek *kata*, and Provençal itself has *cadauns*, *cadaus*.

---

[33] Cf. Jeanroy, vol. 2, pps. 178-182.

[34] The change of *c'r* to *ir* occurs with an early syncopation of the weak post-tonic vowel *e*; if, on the other hand, this vowel is kept, as is so often the case in Provençal, we get an assibilation of the intervocalic prepalatal *k*. Cf. CL *nŏcĕre* > VL * *nŏcĕre* > *noire* and *nózer*.

2. PEIRE VIDAL

Peire Vidals si fo de Tolosa. Fils fo d'un pelicer. E cantava meilz c'ome del mon. E fo dels plus fols omes que mais fossen; qu'el crezia que tot fos vers so que a lui plazia ni qu'el volia. E plus leu li avenia tobars que a nuil home del mon, e fo aquels que plus rics sons fetz e majors fulias dis d'armas e d'amor e de mal dir d'autrui. E fo vers c'us cavaliers de San Zili li tailla la lenga, per so qu'el donava ad entendre qu'el era drutz de sa muiller. E.N Us del Baus si.l fetz garir e medegar. E quant fo garritz, el s'en anet outra mar. De lai el amenet una Grega, que.il fo donada a muiller en Cypry. E.ill fo dat a entendre qu'ela era neza de l'emperador de Constantinopoli, e qu'el per lei devia aver l'emperi per rason. Don el mes tot quant poc gazaingnar a far navilli, qu'el crezia anar l'emperi conquistar. E.n portava armas emperials e fasia se clamar emperaire e la muiller emperariz.

Peire Vidals si fo de Tolosa. Fils fo d'un pelicer. 'Peire Vidal was from Toulouse. He was the son of a furrier.'

Peire. This asigmatic nominative (not ending in -*s*) cannot go back to Lat. *Pĕtrus*, but follows the imparisyllabic flexion of *bar - baró(n)* (< *báro - baróne*): *Peire - Peiró(n)*, a flexion which seems to have originated from an Old Frankish declension in -*o*, -*un* (*háno - hánun*; *Húgo - Húgun*), adapted to the stress pattern of the Lat. -*o*, -*one* type (*látro - latróne*) insofar as the Germanic flexion itself did not involve any shift in stress, as seen from the avobe examples. Germanic proper names of this type are frequent in Provençal: *Carles - Carlon*; *Uc - Ugon*; *Ebles - Eblon*, etc. [35] The nominative is usually *Peire*, seldom *Peires* with an analogical -*s* (cf. *lo bar* and *lo bars* < *baro*); the accusative, on the other hand, seems to be more frequently *Peire* than *Peiró(n)*; cf. *ab Peire de Monzo* (HAMLIN, 46, 43). The great fluctuation in treatment stems from the hybrid nature of this proper name.

pelicer is derived from *pĕllīceus* 'consisting of furs.' The agent suffix is either -*er* or -*ier*; the Anglade version has *pelissier*. *Peletier* (Fr. *pelletier*) comes from medieval Lat. *pelletarius*. [36]

E cantava meilz c'ome del mon. 'And he sang better than anybody in the world.'

meilz < *mĕlius.* The Anglade edition has *mielhs*, showing the optional diphthongization caused by yod; *il* and *lh* both represent

---

[35] For a discussion of the flexion in -*one*, see Rohlfs, p. 114; and, with great detail and acumen, Crescini, p. 69.
[36] Cf. REW 6375 *pĕllīceus*.

a palatalized *l*. There is no rigorous distinction in Provençal between final *s* and final *z*: *fils* and *filz*, etc., while French has *z* after a palatal *l* only, not after a non-palatal *l*.

meilz c'ome. Logically, one would expect a nominative case in a comparative clause, as in the following example, from Boutière, p. 263, 62-63: *En Pons de Cabdueill fo plus alegres que hom del mon*. The preposition *de* was also used to introduce a comparison (cf. the Anglade version which here has: *mielhs d'home*), and it is entirely possible that the accusative used here stems from a contamination with this construction, but the accusative is by no means infrequent in comparisons introduced by *que*.

mon < *mŭndu* represents the popular development (cf. Old Fr. *mont*); a learned form *monde* is quoted in Levy's dictionary.

E fo dels plus fols omes que mais fossen; qu'el crezia que tot fos vers so que a lui plazia ni qu'el volia. 'And he was one of the craziest men that ever lived, for he thought that everything was true so long as it pleased him or he wanted it.'

dels < *de ĭllos*. Provençal does not drop the *l* in contractions involving a preposition and the definite article in the plural: *als* < *ad ĭllos*; *pels* < *per ĭllos*. Compare the stronger contraction in Fr. *des* and Old Fr. *as*.

fossen < *fŭissent* with *-en* as a regular continuation of Lat. *-ent*. An analogical ending *-on*, from Lat. *-unt*, is quite common: *fosson*; cf. *cantant* > *cantan* and, with analogical endings, *canton* and *canten*.

crezia < *crede(b)at* shows the regular development of intervocalic *d* to a voiced *s* and has the normal imperfect ending *-ia* from *-e(b)at*. The presence of a subjunctive, *fos* < *fŭisset*, indicates that we have to do with a false belief. This same modal usage is found in Old French.

vers is regularly derived from CL *vērus*. Provençal also has a continuation of VL *veracu > *verai*, Fr. *vrai*: *tant es sos pretz verais e fis* (Jaufré Rudel).

so < *ecce-(h)ŏc*, with *e* becoming a yod in hiatus with *o*. Proof of the early reduction of *ts* (< *kį*) to *s* is evident in the standard graph of this word; compare also spellings such as *sert* (< *cĕrtu*), *sercar* (< *cĭrcare*).

ni does not convey any negative meaning here; it is a coordinating conjunction which often means 'or' or 'and.'

E plus leu li avenia trobars que a nuil home del mon 'and writing poetry came easier to him than to anybody else in the world.'

leu < *lĕve*. Final *v* is vocalized to *u̯* in Provençal: *nave* > *nau*; *clave* > *clau*; *brĕve* > *breu*. An optional diphthongization of *ĕ* to *ie* and *ŏ* to *uo, ue* occurs with final *-u*, not only with primary *-u*: *dĕu* > *deu, dieu*; *mĕu* > *meu, mieu*, but also with the secondary *-u* obtained from the vocalization of *v*: *lĕve* > *leu, lieu, brĕve* > *breu, brieu*; CL *ōvu* > VL *ŏvu* > *ou, uou, ueu*.

li < *ĭllī* is a weak dative form, unchangeable in gender just like Old Fr. *li*.

trobars. When used substantivally, the infinitive normally requires the definite article (or the equivalent) in Old French (*li perdres, le morir*), but although Anglade quotes all substantival forms of the infinitive in Provençal with the article (*lo chantars, lo volers*), this appendage is not at all obligatory as any extended reading will easily testify.[37] When used as a noun, the infinitive is modeled on the *murs - mur type* declension: *lo trobars - lo trobar*, with a flexional *s* added in the nominative. An example of the accusative: *el perdet lo vezer e l'auzir*.

nuil is the equivalent of *nulh*, *il* being a graph for palatalized *l*. *Nūllu* gives *nul*; the palatalization must be of analogical origin, and a variety of explanations has been offered to solve this problem. A regional, yet widespread palatalization of *l* in the *-llī* ending would give us *nūllī* > *nulh*, from where the palatal could spread to other forms of the word. These regions, which include the Limousin, have

---

[37] Cf. Anglade, p. 221.

other nominative plurals in *-lh*: *caballī* > *cavalh*; *ĭllī* > *ilh*. Some confusion could arise from suffixes such as *-alh, -ilh, -elh* (< *-aculu, -īculu, -ĭculu*), with a palatalized *l* spreading to words which etymologically have *l*. Appel suggests influence of a * *nūllia* created with *omnia* as a model. [38]

e fo aquels que plus rics sons fetz e majors fulias dis d'armas e d'amor e de mal dir d'autrui. 'and he was the one who wrote the most harmonious poetry and who told the tallest stories of battles and love affairs and slanders.'

aquels (*aquel* in the Anglade edition) < * *accu-ĭlle*, representing a combination of *eccu* and *ac* or *atque* plus *ĭlle*. The regular nom. sing. form is *aquel* (cf. *ecce-ĭste* > *cest*; *ecce-ĭlle* > *cel*), the difference from French being that Provençal does not, in the singular, have any change to * *ecce-ĭstī*, * *ecce-ĭllī*, with the resulting *umlaut* change of *e* to *i* (cf. Old Fr. *cist, cil*). Sigmatic forms (*aquels, cels*) are not uncommon in the nom. sing.; they draw their *-s* from the masculine flexion.

plus < *plūs*. An alternating form *pus* is usually explained as stemming from a dissimilation process in such combinations as *plus leu, plus lonc, plus larc* or *lo plus* from where it then spreads to a more general use. It is found over wide areas of Romania.

sons refers to the music that accompanies the poems. The troubadours attached the greatest importance to the purely formal aspects of versification and musical rhythm, and they were constantly striving to achieve perfection in their dual role as poets and composers.

fulias. The normal form is *folias*, but the trend towards a closure of *o* to *u* in pretonic position is prevalent over wide areas of

---

[38] Cf. Grandgent, § 67, 2; and Appel, § 49. Grafström (Morph., § 43) endorses Appel's explanation of the palatalization feature. Provençal also has a form, *lhuŋ*, obtained from *nulh* through a reciprocal metathesis which may have been touched off by other negations and indefinite pronouns ending in *-un*: *negun, degun, alcun. Lhun* may, in turn, become *lunh* through a metathesis of the palatal element; cf. *no fam lunha differensa* 'we establish no difference' (Appel: Chr., 124, 71).

Romance; cf. *lŏcale* > Sp. *lugar*; *iŏcare* > Sp. *jugar*; *pŏrtare* > Rm. *purtá*.[39]

dis < *dīxit* is the 3. pers. sing. of the perf. ind. The ending *-it* is lost early; compare Old Fr. *dist* where *t* remains after the loss of *i*.

dir. *Dīcĕre* > *diire* > *dire*, with *e* retained as a supporting vowel for the *c'r* cluster and with the yod absorbed by the preceding vowel *i*; the form *dir* is drawn by analogy from the *-ire* conjugation (*auzir, venir,* etc.).

autrui. Modeled on the relative pronoun *cui*, Vulgar Latin creates the tonic masc. personal pronoun *illui* (> *lui*) which, in turn, leads to the formation of demonstrative pronouns in *-ui*: *cellui, selhuy,* Fr. *celui* and Old Fr. *cestui*. A couple of indefinite pronouns were subject to similar developments: Pr. Fr. *autrui* and It. *altrui* are drawn from *autre* and *altro* respectively, and Old French develops *nului* and a dissimilated *nelui* from *nul*.

E fo vers c'us cavaliers de San Zili li tailla la lenga 'and it was true that a knight from Saint-Gilles cut his tongue out.'

San Zili. *Aegidius*, with loss of the initial diphthong, gives Old Fr. *Gires* and a collateral form *Giles*, now spelled *Gilles*. *Zili* represents an unusual development for Provençal of a prepalatal *g*, since *g + e, i* normally gives [dž] (other manuscripts have *San Gili* here). Appel points out that we do not have exact proof of the pronunciation [dž] to begin with, but that we assume it "ohne genauere Begründung."[40] In fact, following a liquid, Provençal admits both [dž] and [dz], spelled *g* and *z* respectively: *bŭrgēnse* > *borges, borzes*; *sŭrgĕre* > *sorger, sorzer*; *fŭlgŭre* > *fŭlgĕre > *folger, folzer*. Most probably, [dz] represents a more recent development of [dž], and conditions in Provençal would seem to indicate that this further change occurred essentially where *g* followed

---

[39] Cf. Lausberg, §§ 253-255.

[40] Cf. Appel, § 44c; and Grafström, § 62, 2. Crescini (p. 24) mentions only the standard development to [dž].

a liquid. It is not attested elsewhere in Provençal texts of the classical period, and our example conforms to this rule insofar as *San Zili* is to be considered a single phonetic unit. The development of prepalatal *g* to [*dz*] is a characteristic feature of Northern Italian dialects where it also occurs in absolute initial position: Piemontese *ẓənuju* (< *gĕnŭcŭlu*); *ẓenu* (< *gĕneru*), and for Lunigiana *ẓenta* (< *gĕnte*); *ẓenero* (< *gĕneru*). In all these examples, *ẓ* is the equivalent of [*dz*].[41] The special development in Old French of a few words which change intervocalic *dį* to *rį* has not been sufficiently explained; it is characteristic of the words involved that they are not of a popular nature: *mĕdicu* > **mĕdiu* > Old Fr. *mire*; *ĭnvĭdia* > Old Fr. *envirie, envire*; *remĕdiu* > Old Fr. *remire*; *grammaticu* > **grammadiu* > Fr. *grammaire*. Nyrop mentions the brief existence in Old French of collateral forms in *l* which all disappear with the exception of *Gilles* which completely replaces *Gires*.[42] Provençal, interestingly enough, shows the *l* stage of this development: *Zili, navilli*. The retention of a syllabic final *i* is characteristic of learned words: *Zilli, Cypry, emperi, fluvi*, etc.

tailla. In French, the weak perfects of the *-are* conjugation are derived from a reduced Vulgar Latin form where *v* is lost: *cantavit* > **cantāt* > *chanta*, as opposed to It. *cantò*, Sp. *cantó*, Pg. *cantou* which are derived from VL **cantaut*, with vocalization of *v* to *u̯*. This French type perfect has left little trace in Provençal where it is rarely found outside of the troubadour biographies, and it occurs only in the 3. pers. sing. It also exists in Old Catalan, and Grafström has encountered one instance of it (*presta*) in a deed from Toulouse.[43]

lenga < *lĭngua*. *Lengua* is nothing more than a graphical variant; the sound is [*g*], resulting from a simplification of the original [*gw*] cluster.

---

[41] For conditions in Northern Italian dialects, consult Rohlfs: Hist. Gr., §§ 156 and 158; and for examples of palatal *g* following a liquid (ex. *plangĕre* > Lomb., Ven. *pianśer*), ib., §§ 256 and 264. For a general presentation of *ge-, gi-* in Romance, see Lausberg, §§ 323-324.

[42] For this problem in Old French, see Nyrop, vol. 1, § 475, 4, Rem.; and Rheinfelder, § 751.

[43] Cf. Lausberg, § 824; Grafström: Morph., § 65, a; and, for Catalan, Badía Margarit, § 164.

per so qu'el donava ad entendre qu'el era drutz de sa muiller. 'because he pretended to be his wife's lover.'

donava. Provençal has kept CL *dare,* but has also adopted the Gallo-Romance form *donare* which takes the place of *dare* in Northern France; cf. *fo donada* alternating in this text with *fo dat.*

ad entendre. Our text also has *a entendre* instead of the etymologically correct *az entendre. Ad* is closely linked with *entendre* with which it forms one phonetic group, and *d,* rather than final, is thus in an intervocalic position and should go to a voiced *s*. There are, however, numerous cases in Provençal of the retention as well as of the loss of *d* in intervocalic position. In *a entendre,* we may have an analogy from *ad* used before a word beginning with a consonant. [44]

drutz. Rohlfs derives *drutz* from a Gaulish word * *druto* 'strong, powerful,' while Gamillscheg suggests an Old Frankish * *drûd* as the etymology. [45]

muiller < VL *mŭliére* < *mŭlierem.* The vowel combinations *ie* and *io* of Classical Latin were subject to a change in stress in Vulgar Latin: *ie* > *ié*; *io* > *ió*, with the accent shifting to the more open of the two vowels. The vowel *i* then became a yod, capable of palatalizing the preceding consonant: *mŭliére* > *molhér.* A close pronunciation of pretonic *o* is reflected in the frequent spelling *u* (cf. *folias* and *fulias*), yet *molher* is more common than *mulher.* Compare Sp. *mujer* where the closure of *o* is brought about by the palatal (cf. *cōgnatu* > Sp. *cuñado*).

E.N Us del Baus si.l fetz garir e medegar. 'and Uc des Baux had him treated and restored to health.'

.N. The title *en,* frequent in Provençal where it replaces *don, dom,* is drawn from the final syllable of *dŏmĭne.* Chabaneau and

---

[44] For the fluctuating treatment of intervocalic *d,* see Crescini, pps. 41-42. For a similar fluctuation in Spanish (ex. *sūdōre* > *sudor*; *audīre* > *oír*), consult Menéndez Pidal, § 41, 2.

[45] Cf. Rohlfs, p. 160 and notes 425, 426; E. Gamillscheg: *Romania Germanica,* Berlin-Leipzig, 1934, p. 226; and REW 2779b *drutos.*

Schultz-Gora derive *en* from *-ne* through a false resolution of combinations like *den* and *quen* (*de ne Peire, que ne Peire* > *den P., quen P.*) *Ne* from *domine* is parallel to *na* from *domina*: *domna Maria* > *na Maria*. The form *ne* is used before a vowel or before *h*: *ne Helias*; *n'* also occurs before a vowel: *n'Uc del Bauç*, but elsewhere, the standard form is *en*. *E.N* contains the enclitic form of the title.[46]

Us. The Germanic nominative *Húgo* gives *Uc* which, adapted to the *murs - mur* flexion, can give us either *Ucs* or, with the loss of *c* before flexional *s*, *Us*.

garir < * *warjan*. Germanic verbs in *-jan* normally join the *-ire* conjugation. Old French also has *garir*; the modern form *guérir* is an example of the fluctuation, in many areas of Romania, between *er* and *ar*: Old Fr. *lerme* > Fr. *larme*; CL *separare* > VL *seperare*.

medegar < *mědĭcāre*. The weak intertonic vowel is kept here, and *c* has voiced to *g* in intervocalic position, but the weak vowel *ĭ* of the *-ĭcāre* suffix may also drop, giving *metjar* or *metgar*, voiced results that point to a late syncopation which would permit a voicing of *c*. The pronunciation is [dž] in *metjar*, [g] in *metgar*, and this difference corresponds to the treatment of initial *ca-* and *ga-*; where these are kept intact (ex: *carrĭcare* > *cargar*), we have [g], where they are palatalized (ex.: *carrĭcare* > *charjar*), we have [dž].[47]

E quant fo garritz, el s'en anet outra mar. 'And when he recovered, he went overseas.'

garritz is but a graphical variant of *garitz*; final *t's* is regularly spelled *tz*.

anet. An unusual feature of Provençal verb morphology is the spread of perfects in open *e* into the *-are* conjugation. It is a well-

---

[46] For a detatiled discussion of the origin of *en*, see Crescini, pps. 129-135; and articles by A. Thomas, in *Romania*, vol. 12, pps. 585-587, and E. Richter, in *ZRPh*, vol. 27, p. 193 ff.

[47] See Crescini, p. 26; and Anglade, p. 165, for a discussion of this dialectal distribution.

established fact that the rare Latin perfects in -ēvī (delēvī, complēvī) are not continued in Romance, that verbs with an e stem draw their perfect from dědī: CL pérdĭdī > VL perdḗdĭ through a process of recomposition (shift of stress from prefix to stem and restoration of original vowel). VL perdḗdī > perdei or perdiei, with the second d lost through dissimilation and with optional diphthongization. Although this perfect formation in dědī is found also in French: Old Fr. perdiet, vendiet, and Italian: andiede, Provençal alone will generalize its use in the -are conjugation, treating cantẹi like vendẹi.[48] The origin of anar (and Fr. aller) has been much debated, but Rohlfs expresses his faith in ambulare as the common etymon for the various Romance developments. Corominas concludes rather more philosophically that, since all the etymologies that have been proposed, are deficient in one way or another, it is perhaps better to limit oneself to ambulare rather than to operate with various other possibilities such as * ambitare and * adnare. The greatest hurdle is to get from ambulare to * amlare, since the insertion of a b in the m'l cluster is a regular phonetic feature of Gallo-Romance (cf. sĭmŭlāre > semblar, Fr. sembler). If one accepts, with Corominas, that this is possible through careless pronunciation, then the road is open for further changes: * amlare > allare (assimilation of ml to ll) > Fr. aller, or * amlare > amnare (attested in an inscription from Carthage and obtained through an assimilation of the nasality feature) > anar (Provençal reduces mn to n: somnare > sonar).[49]

---

[48] Cf. Crescini, pps. 116-117; Lausberg, § 894; and Rohlfs: Hist. Gr., § 579. For the survival, in the biographies, of the -avi perfect, see above tailla.

[49] Cf. Corominas, art. andar; and REW 412 ambŭlāre. Contrasting with Rohlfs' firm conviction that only one etymon is required for Pr. Cat. anar, Fr. aller, Sp. andar and It. andare: "Es darf heute als gesichert gelten, dass alle diese Formen auf lateinisch ambulare beruhen" (Rohlfs, p. 83), von Wartburg states, as his personal opinion, that all attempts to derive aller and andare from the same source have failed: "Die versuche, allar und andare als gleichen ursprungs aufzufassen, müssen als gescheitert betrachtet werden" (FEW, art. ambulare). VL ambulare and even alare, an ulterior development of ambulare, are both attested in the Glossary of Reichenau: isset - ambulasset; incedentes - ambulantes; transgredere - ultra alare; transiliuit - trans alavit. Malkiel (Malkiel, Y. Linguistica Generale, Filologia Romanza, Etimologia. Firenze: Sansoni, 1970, p. 137), another exponent of a monogenetic explanation, favors * ambitare as the common etymon, even though it fails

De lai el amenet una Grega, qu.il fo donada a muiller en Cypry. 'From there, he brought back a Greek woman whom he had married on Cyprus.'

lai < (*ĭl*)*lac*. Final *c* is either changed to *i̯* or dropped after *a*: *lai, la*; *(ec)ce-(h)ac* > *sai, sa*.

.il (and also *.ill*) is the enclitic form of the weak dative pronoun *li*.

Cypry. Old French likewise had *Cypre*, showing a normal phonological evolution of prepalatal *c*; cf. Engl. *Cyprus*. Fr. *Chypre* has come in via It. *Cipro*. *Y* is learned spelling.

E.ill fo dat a entendre qu'ela era neza de l'emperador de Constantinopoli, e qu'el per lei devia aver l'emperi per rason. 'And he was given to understand that she was the niece of the emperor of Constantinople, and that through her, he was the rightful heir to the empire.'

neza < *nĕptia*. The *ti̯* cluster is assibilated to [*ts*], spelled *z*, then reduced to *s*, which explains the forms *nesa* and *nessa*. *P* is lost before the *ti̯* group as compared with the retention of liquids in the same position: *fŏrtia* > *forza, forsa*. The form *nepsa* appears to be drawn from the masculine *neps* < *nĕpos*.

lei < (*il*)*lei*. VL *illeius* and *illei* are created on the basis of *eius, ei* and become feminine pronouns under the influence of the dative *illae*. Like masc. *illuius, illui* to which they form a parallel, *illeius* and *illei* are attested in Roman inscriptions. Provençal has both *lei* and *leis* and also uses *ela, ella*, all tonic forms appearing after a preposition: *ab lieys, per lei, d'ela, ad ella*.[50]

rason < *ratiōne*. Intervocalic *ti̯* gives a voiced *s*; unlike French, there is not normally any release of yod in Provençal: * *bĕllatiōre*

---

to account for the French development which is seen as having suffered an undetermined associative interference.

[50] Cf. Rohlfs, p. 62. For a detailed presentation of this difficult problem, see Crescini, p. 79; for It. *lei* see Rohlfs: Hist. Gr., § 441.

> *belazor*; *prĕtiāre* > *prezar*, although this development is encountered sporadically: *raizó*, *saizó* (< *satiōne*).'

Don el mes tot quant poc gazaingnar a far navilli, qu'el crezia anar l'emperi conquistar. 'Consequently, he spent all his earnings on the construction of ships, for he intended to set out to conquer the empire.'

mes < *mĭsit*. CL *mīsit* has undergone analogical influence from the past participle *mĭssu*, which accounts for the short *i*. Rohlfs mentions various compromise solutions in Italian dialects between these two forms, the perfect and the past participle, since they are frequently built on the same root: Florentine *messi*, Old Paduan *missi*, etc.[51]

poc < *pŏtuit*. The development is normal, with loss of *t* before the *ui* cluster.

gazaingnar is from Germanic **waidanjan* and is an important exception to the rule that *-jan* verbs join the *-ire* conjugation; it becomes a first conjugation verb in Romance. The Germanic diphthong *ai* is reduced to *a*, and *d* has undergone regular intervocalic treatment to a voiced *s*.

navilli. FEW, art. *navĭgium* has, for Provençal, *navei* and *naveg*, quotes *navili* as a hapax (one single occurrence), and lists, for Old French, *navilie*, *navirie*, *navire*, *navie*. *Navilli* as well as the French forms in *l* and *r*) is semi-learned as pointed out above (under *San Zili*), where we discussed this particular development of *dį*; a hypothetic Vulgar Latin **navidiu* for *navigiu* would account for the evolution of this particular word, and this is, in fact, the solution proposed by Michaelsson.[52]

conquistar. CL *conquirĕre* > VL *conquaerĕre* (recomposition of compound verb) > *conquerre*, and also *conquerir* with a change in

---

[51] Cf. Rohlfs: Hist. Gr., § 585.
[52] For an excellent discussion of this development, see FEW, art. *navĭgium*.

conjugation (compare for French *querre - quérir*; *corre - courir*). *Conquistar* is built on the past participle *conquest, conquist*; *quest* constitutes the phonological outcome of VL *quaestu* (cf. It. *chiesto*), which replaces CL *quaesītu*, while *quist* is based on an analogy with the perfect (*quis*) with which, as has already been observed, the past participle is closely linked.

E.n portava armas emperials e fasia se clamar emperaire e la muiller emparariz. 'And he carried imperial weapons and referred to himself as emperor and to his wife as empress.'

.n is the enclitic form of *ĭnde*, a weak word which has suffered a strong reduction.

e fasia se clamar. A weak pronoun cannot begin a sentence nor does it, as a rule, follow immediately after the coordinating conjunction *e* in Provençal; instead, it is placed after the verb. This same syntax also obtains for Old French.

emperaire - emparariz. The masc. nom. sing. is *emperaire* < *ĭmperātor*, and the acc. is *emperador* < *ĭmperatōre*; the nominative is used here after *se clamar*. The fem. *ĭmperatrīce* usually gives *emperairitz*; *emparariz* shows *a* for *e*, which may be considered a phenomenon of assimilation or vowel harmony. A similar form is attested for Latin in an inscription from Bulgaria: *pro salute Iparatori Agusti*. The *a* for *ai* may represent a reduction of a diphthong in a weak intertonic position, or else it may be ascribed to an analogy from masc. *emperador*.[53]

---

[53] A rather common feature of Provençal is the reduction of pretonic or intertonic (and even tonic) diphthongs to a single vowel. Grafström offers only one example of intertonic *ai* > *a*: *Balazvila* alternating with *Balaidsvila*, from Gothic * *Balahaidis*, but the list has been extended by M. Pfister who, in addition, quotes hypercorrect forms like *Figairet* for *Figaret* < *ficarētu*. Cf. Grafström, § 5, 2; and M. Pfister, in *Vox Romanica*, vol. 17, 1958, pps. 291-292. *Fraidel - fradel* (< Germanic * *freidi*) may serve as an example of the same alternance in pretonic position: *fradel* is already encountered in the *Sainte Foi d'Agen*: *paupras laissed cuma fradelz* (v. 99). Cf. REW 3490 *freidi*.

3. RAZÓ (BERTRAN DE BORN: POIS LO GENS TERMINIS FLORIS)

Lo reis Enrics d'Englaterra si tenia assis En Bertran de Born dedins Autafort e.l combatia ab sos edeficis, que molt li volia grand mal, car el crezia que tota la guerra que.l reis Joves, sos fillz, l'avia faicha, qu'En Bertrans la.il agues faita far; e per so era vengutz denant Autafort per lui desiritar. E.l reis d'Arragon venc en l'ost del rei Enric denant Autafort. E cant Bertrans o saub, si fo molt alegres que.l reis d'Arragon era en l'ost, per so qu'el era sos amics especials. E.l reis d'Arragon si mandet sos messatges dinz lo castel, qu'En Bertrans li mandes pan e vin e carn; et el si l'en mandet assatz. E per lo messatge per cui el mandet los presenz, el li mandet pregan qu'el fezes si qu'el fezes mudar los edeficis e far traire en autra part, que.l murs on il ferion era tot rotz. Et el per gran aver del rei Enric, el li dis tot so qu'En Bertrans l'avia mandat a dir. E.l reis Enrics si fetz metre dels edificis plus en aquella part on saup que.l murs era rotz, e fon lo murs ades per terra e.l castels pres.

En Bertrans ab tota sa gen fon menatz al pabaillon del rei Enric, e.l reis lo receup molt mal. E.l reis Enrics si.l dis: "Bertrans, Bertrans, vos avetz dig que anc la meitatz del vostre sen no.us ac mestier nulls temps, mas sapchatz qu'ara vos a el ben mestier totz." "Seingner, dis En Bertrans, el es ben vers qu'eu o dissi, e dissi ben vertat." E.l rei dis: "Eu cre ben qu'el vos sia aras faillitz." "Seingner, dis En Bertrans, ben m'es faillitz." "E com?" dis lo reis. "Seingner, dis En Bertrans, lo jorn que.l valens Joves reis, vostre fillz, mori, eu perdei lo sen e.l saber e la conoissensa." E.l reis, quant auzi so qu'En Bertrans li dis en ploran, del fil, venc li granz dolors al cor, de pietat, et als oills, si que no.is poc tener qu'el

non pasmes de dolor. E quant el revenc de pasmazon, el crida e
dis en ploran: "En Bertrans, En Bertrans, vos avetz ben drech, et
es ben razos, si vos avetz perdut lo sen per mon fill, qu'el vos volia
meils que ad home del mon. Et eu, per amor de lui, vos quit la
persona e l'aver e.l vostre castel e vos ren la mia amor e la mia
gracia, e vos don cinc cenz marcs d'argen per los dans que vos
avetz receubutz." En Bertrans si.l cazec als pes, referrent li gracias
e merces. E.l reis ab tota la soa ost s'en anet.

    En Bertrans, can saup que.l reis d'Arragon l'avia faita si laida
fellonia, fon molt iratz ab lo rei N'Anfos. E si sabia com era
vengutz al rei Enric esser soudadiers logaditz e sabia com lo reis
d'Arragon era vengutz de paubra generacion de Carlades, d'un castel
que a nom Carlat, que es en la seingnoria del comte de Rodes.
E.N Peire de Carlat, qu'era seingner del castel, per valor e per
proessa, si pres per moiller la comtessa d'Amillau, qu'era caseguda
en eretat, e si n'ac un fil, que fon valens e pros, e conquis lo comtat
de Proenssa. Et us sos fils si conquis lo comtat de Barsalona et ac
nom Raimons Berrengiers, lo quals conquis lo regisme d'Arragon
e fo lo premiers reis que anc fos en Arragon. E anet penre corona
a Roma; e cant s'en tornava e fon al borc Saint Dalmas, el mori.
E remanseron ne trei fill: Anfos, lo quals fo reis d'Arragon, aquest
que fetz lo mal d'En Bertran de Born, e l'autre, don Sancho, et
l'autre, Berrengiers de Besaudunes. E saup com el avia traïda la
filla de l'emperador Manuel, que l'emperaire l'avia mandada per
moiller ab grant tresor et ab grant aver et ab molt honrada compaingnia, e los raubet de tot l'aver que la domna e.ill Grec avian;
e com los enviet per mar, marritz e consiros e desconseillatz, e com
sos fraire Sanchos l'avia touta Proenssa, e com s'esperjuret, per
l'aver que.l reis Enrics li det, contra.l comte de Tolosa. E de totas
aquestas razons fetz En Bertrans de Born lo sirventes que ditz:
Pois lo gens terminis floris.

Lo reis Enrics d'Englaterra si tenia assis En Bertran de Born dedins Autafort e.l combatia ab sos edeficis, que molt li volia grand mal 'King Henry of England was laying siege to Bertran de Born in Hautefort and was fighting against him with all his military machines, determined to inflict great harm on him.'

assis, a past participle derived from *ad* + *sedēre*, does not continue CL *sessum*, but owes its vowel *i* to an analogy with *mis* and *pris*. These participles, however, are in no way regular phonological developments either, since *mĭssu* gives *mes* and *pre(h)ē(n)su pres*. *Mis* is relatively rare: its vowel may originate from an analogy with the perfect *mīsī*, changing *mĭssu* into ** mīsu > mis*. The parallelism between the past participle and the perfect may be observed in many other participles: *asses* and *assis*, *ques* and *quis*, *conques* and *conquis*, etc., and compare also *dit*, *dig* (< CL *dĭctu*) which draws its vowel from *dis* (< *dīxī*), as opposed to a phonological *detto* in Italian. *Mis* and *pris* are usually considered to be French borrowings rather than alternate developments within Provençal, probably because of their rare occurrence in the South. [54]

dedins and *dinz* are derived from *(de) de ĭntus*, which regularly gives forms in *e*: *dentz*, *dens*; *ĭntus > ens, entz*. The combination of *nt* + consonant constitutes an insufficient condition for weakening *e* to *i*, a development which occurs only if, in addition, the vowel is pretonic: *ĭntrāre > intrar*, but these two factors are combined here

---

[54] Lausberg (§ 917) mentions the analogy from the perfect for Fr. *mis*, *pris*, *quis*, but not for Provençal. Influenced by the perfect are Old It. *miso*, Emilian *miss*, Lunigiano *miso*, Lucchese and Pisan *misso*; see Rohlfs: Hist. Gr., § 625.

because of the prevalent proclitic status of prepositions. *Dens, ens* then are stressed forms, *dins, ins* are weak.⁵⁵

edeficis, from Lat. *ædĭfĭcium*, shows a learned retention of the penult; cf. *servizi, sacrifici*. Most Classical Latin neuter nouns in *-um* changed to the masculine declension in Vulgar Latin, adopting the *-us* ending. This change is well attested in popular writers such as Petronius who has *vinus, balneus, vasus*, etc., and Plautus who uses *dorsus, corius*, etc. (for CL *vinum, balneum*, etc.). Since neuters in *-um* form a plural in *-a* in Classical Latin, a considerable number of neuter plurals become feminine singulars in Vulgar Latin because of the *-a* morpheme, and quite frequently, both forms survive, the singular as a masculine, the plural as a feminine noun. Examples of this: *fŏliu > folh*, Old Fr. *fueil*, It. *foglio*; *fŏlia > folha*, Fr. *feuille*, It. *foglia*; *granu > gra*, Fr. *grain*; *grana > grana*, Fr. *graine*; *pratu > prat*; * *prata > prada*.⁵⁶

li < ĭllī is an unstressed dative form. Before a vowel, it is elided to *l'*: *la filla ... que l'emperaire l'avia mandada*. The enclitic dative is either *.il* (*.ill*) or *.l*: *la.il agues faita far*; *si.l dis*.

car el crezia que tota la guerra que.l reis Joves, sos fillz, l'avia faicha, qu'En Bertrans la.il agues faita far; e per so era vengutz denant Autafort per lui desiritar. 'For he thought that the whole war that the Young King, his son, had started against him, was because Bertran had made him start it; and therefore he had come to besiege Hautefort with the purpose of depriving him of his inheritance'.

.l reis Joves. The young King is Henri au Court Mantel (1155-1183), oldest son of Henry II Plantagenet.

---

⁵⁵ Cf. Grafström, § 9, 2; and specifically G. Millardet: "A propos de provençal *dins*", in *RLR*, vol. 57, 1914, pps. 189-203. Millardet points to four factors that must combine in order to produce the change of *e* to *i* (three of which are grouped together here): 1. the vowel must be initial; 2. it must appear before three consonants; 2. it must be immediately followed by a nasal; and 4. it must be unstressed.

⁵⁶ For the fate of the neuter gender in Vulgar Latin, see Väänänen, §§ 213-225.

faicha < *facta* contains a purely graphical *i*; our text also has the alternate form *faita*.

agues < *habuisset*. The use of the subjunctive after *crezia* points to a false belief. A similar example with *cujar* (< *cogitare*): *enans me cuiava de vos qu'en Bascols de Cotanda fos* (Appel: Chr., 5, 351-52). In the following example, from Boutière, p. 242, 25-28, the context clearly shows that we have to do with a false belief: *Et ella sentit lo baizar e crezet qu'el fos En Barrals, sos maritz, e rizen ela se levet. E garda e vit qu'el era.l fol de Peire Vidal*.

per lui desiritar. The tonic form of the pronoun shows its dependence on the preposition; cf. this example: *e per voluntat de leis vezer* (Hamlin, 16,4), with tonic *leis* and not an unstressed *la*. This construction also represents the norm in Old French whereas, in modern French, a weak pronoun is used, completely divorced from the preposition and functioning as the direct object of the infinitive: Old Fr. *de lui querre* becomes modern Fr. *de le chercher*. While this particular syntax seems to represent the norm in Provençal, we also find a different type construction in which the pronoun, in its weak form, is placed after the preposition + infinitive combination where it can escape a direct dependence on the preposition: *e comenzet los a menassar fortmen de deseretar los e de destruire los* (Stimming, 14, 9-10). A strong pronoun may occasionally appear in that position: *senes veser leis* (Hamlin, 32, 12), or the pronoun may even be omitted altogether: *et enamoret se de la comtessa de Tripol ses vezer* (Hamlin, 16, 2). The use of the weak pronoun, placed between the preposition and the infinitive, is, no doubt, a rare occurrence: *e pois montet a caval ses le vezer* (Boutière, p. 209, 9). [57]

desiritar and *eretat*. CL *hērēdǐtāre* > *eretar* and *eritar*, a variant which may have originated through vocalic dissimilation. French has *hériter* and not * *hereter,* but compare Sp. *heredar* and Old Fr. *heretaige*. [58]

---

[57] For this syntax, see Schultz-Gora, § 177; and consult Foulet (§§ 182-183) for similar constructions in Old French.
[58] See FEW, art. *hērēdǐtas*. Von Wartburg suggests that the vocalic fluctuation may have been touched off by a similar alternance in the suffixes *-ité* and *-eté*: *charité - fermeté*.

E.l reis d'Arragon venc en l'ost del rei Enric denant Autafort. E cant Bertrans o saub, si fo molt alegres que.l reis d'Arragon era en l'ost, per so qu'el era sos amics especials. 'And the King of Aragon joined King Henry's army outside Hautefort. And when Bertran learned that, he was very happy that the King of Aragon was in the army, because he was a close friend of his'.

Autafort. Pr. *aut* < *altu* is free of any immixture of Germanic * *hoh* (German *hoch*); cf. *altu* + * *hoh* > Fr. *haut*, with an aspirated *h*. In some areas of Romania, *altu* was quite frequently combined with *in*: *in* + *altu* > Pr. *naut* and Rm. *(î)nalt*.

cant < *quando* alternates with *can* in this text, which may prove that the reduction of final *-nt* and *-nd* is not completely carried through, nor can any stringent distribution be observed between *nt* and *nd* before a vowel and *n* before a consonant. Cf. *grand mal, grant tresor, grant aver*; and *cant Bertrans, can saup*. All we seem to have is a fluctuating graphical representation.

saub < *sapuit*. Our text also has the form *saup* which shows normal phonological treatment of final *p*. The graph *b* is easily explained on the basis of such verb forms as *saber, saubist, saubem*; it is a mere graph and does not reflect a voiced sound.

si. The role of this adverbial *si* is to introduce the main clause following a preceding subordinate clause. A similar use of *si* is a common feature of Old French.

alegres < VL * *alĕcre* < CL *álacer*. In Vulgar Latin, the stress will normally shift to the vowel that immediately precedes a mute + liquid: CL *cáthĕdra* > VL *cathĕ́dra*; CL *ténĕbras* > VL *tenĕ́bras*. The accent change is thus a regular feature, but the change in vocalic quality, which this word has undergone, remains unexplained. The use of the indicative after an expression of emotion represents the modal norm in the medieval period. The use of the subjunctive appears in French as late as the end of the 16th — the beginning of the 17th century.

E.l reis d'Arragon si mandet sos messatges dinz lo castel, qu'En Bertrans li mandes pan e vin e carn; et el si l'en mandet assatz. E per lo messatge per cui el mandet los presenz, el li mandet pregan qu'el fezes si qu'el fazes mudar los edificis e far traire en autra part, que.l murs on il ferion era tot rotz. 'And the King of Aragon sent his messengers into the castle with the order that Bertran send him bread and wine and meat; and he sent him large quantities. And through the messenger who was in charge of transporting the gifts (provisions), he pleaded with him to see to it that the catapults be moved to another area, for the wall they were pelting had all but tumbled down'.

mandes < *mandasset* < *mandavisset* is an imperfect subjunctive, governed by the order contained in *mandet sos messatges*. Morphologically is to be observed that the open *e* is carried over from the perfect (*mandęi*), replacing a phonological *mandas*.

pan e vin e carn. Provençal and Old French do not normally make use of a partitive article.

assatz does not convey any restrictive meaning here; it translates as 'much, a lot', just as Old Fr. *assez* is most often the equivalent of modern Fr. *beaucoup*.

cui, from Lat. *cui*, is the norm after a preposition; it refers almost exclusively to persons.

traire < VL * *tragĕre* < CL *trahĕre*. The change to * *tragĕre* is probably caused by analogical influence from *agĕre*. The secondary g'r cluster gives yod + r: *lĕgĕre* > *leire*; *frīgĕre* > * *friire* > *frire*.

autra < *altĕra*. Vocalization of the velar type *l* before a consonant is not carried through to the same extent as in French, and it is very difficult to infer any definite rules governing this process. *L* is usually vocalized to *u* before a dental (*t, d, n, s*) and more often following the vowel *a* than *e* and *o*, but retention of *l* also occurs under the very same conditions: *cal(ĭ)du* > *caut* or *calt*; *falsu* > *faus* or *fals*; *altu* > *aut* or *alt*; * *bĕll(ĭ)tāte* > *beutat* or *beltat*. Retention of *l* is the norm almost exclusively in *alba, albergar, cavalgar*. What further complicates matters is the fact that, in numerous cases, *l* may very well be a learned or archaic graph, retained even after a change in pronunciation had taken place. An occasional loss of *l* may also occur: *cop* for *colp* < * *colpu* < *colaphu*; *mot* for *molt* or *mout* < *mŭltu*. A similar instability in the treatment of *l* before a consonant characterizes Hispano-Romance, where vocalization never got beyond the stage of an incipient move. [59]

on < *ŭnde* is an adverb of location. It may sometimes stand for *en cui, ab cui*; cf. *domna on es beutatz*.

ferion is the 3. pers. plur. of the imperfect of *ferir* and is an alternate form of the regular *ferian*. Although Anglade terms the change of *-ian* to *-ion* a weakening, it would seem more natural to ascribe it to a strong analogical influence, which can be traced back, above all, to the present tense where *cantan* confronts three conjugations with an *-on* ending: *vezon, vendon, dormon*, and may itself become *canton*. While *-on* has an unstable *n*, the *n* of *-an* is always kept in order to avoid a confusion between the singular and the plural.

rotz < *rŭptus*. The Classical Latin participle is also continued in Old French and has survived in Fr. *route* < (*vĭa*) *rŭpta*. *Romput* (Fr. *rompu*) is built on the stem *rŭmp-* of *rŭmpĕre* to which *-ūtu* is added; it is not very common in Provençal, while it completely replaces Old Fr. *rot*.

Et el, per gran aver del rei Enric, el li dis tot so qu'En Bertrans l'avia mandat a dir. E.l reis Enrics si fetz metre dels edificis plus en aquella part on saup que.l murs era rotz, e fon lo murs ades per terra e.l castels pres. 'And because of the great resources of King Henry, he told him everything that Bertran had let him know through his messenger. And King Henry had more catapults placed in the area where he knew the wall was crumbling, and the wall was quickly brought down and the castle taken'.

mandat < *mandātu*. The weak past participles are characterized by the following endings: *-at* in the *a* conjugation, *-ut* in the *e* conjugations and *-it* in the *i* conjugation: *cantātu* > *cantat*; CL *habĭtu* > VL * *habūtu* > *avut* or *agut*; CL *perdĭtu* > VL * *perdūtu* > *perdut*; *partītu* > *partit*. The final dental is regularly kept;

---

[59] Cf. Appel, § 56a; and Lausberg, §§ 411-414.

it voices to *d* in the feminine, where *t* is intervocalic: *cantada, aguda, perduda, partida.*

fon is an alternate form of *fo* < *fŭit,* which owes its final consonant to the problem of the unstable *n* in Provençal, an *n* having been "restored" here by mistake. *Fon,* then, is a case of hypercorrection.

En Bertrans ab tota sa gen fon menatz al pabaillon del rei Enric. e.l reis lo receup molt mal. 'And Bertran and all his people were taken to King Henry's tent, and he was given a severe reception'.

gen < *gĕnte* is a collective noun which is used here as a fem. sing. in accordance with its Latin etymon; cf. *entre la franca gen, per tota bona gen, ab la bona gen.* It is also common as a fem. plur., since it normally refers to a plurality; cf. *aquestas gens blancas, vostras ientz, onradas gens.*

fon menatz agrees grammatically with *En Bertrans* and not with the compound subject; cf. *E.l reis ab tota la soa ost s'en anet.*

menatz < *mĭnātus.* The *Glossary of Reichenau* has: *minatur - manatiat,* showing that CL *mĭnarī,* in its original meaning 'to threaten', had been replaced by *mĭnaciāre* (> *menasar*), derived from the noun *mĭnacia* 'threat' (> *menasa*). In its active form in Vulgar Latin (VL *mĭnare* for CL *mĭnārī*), *minare* is attested with the meaning 'to spur a horse, to lead cattle to pasture', the transition in meaning being linked with the fact that this was done by threatening the animals. Apuleius has *minat asinum.* From this specific usage is derived the more general meaning of 'to lead, to conduct, to guide', prevalent in Provençal as well as in French. The vowel assimilation, evident in *manatiat,* is encountered in the *Sainte Eulalie* which has *manatce.*

pabaillon < *papĭliōne.* A regular development of this word occurs in Sp. *pabellón* and Old Fr. *paveillon,* while Pr. *pabalhon* has undergone vocalic assimilation. An alternate form, *pavilhon,* is a borrowing from French, as seen from the treatment of intervocalic *p.*

receup < *recĭpuit* is an example of the same perfect formation as *saup* < *sapuit*, showing a release of *u̯* before *p*.

E.l reis Enrics si.l dis: "*Bertrans, Bertrans, vos avetz dig que anc la meitatz del vostre sen no.us ac mestier nulls temps, mas sapchatz qu'ara vos a el ben mestier totz.*" "*Seingner dis En Bertrans, el es ben vers q'eu o dissi, e dissi ben vertat.*" 'And King Henry said to him: "Bertran, Bertran, you have said that you never needed even half of your good judgment, but bear in mind that now you need all of it." "Lord, said Bertran, it is true that I said it, and I told the truth".'

dig < * *dīctu* < CL *dĭctu*. The change from *ĭ* to *ī* comes about through analogy with the perfect *dīxī* with possible additional influence of the infinitive *dīcĕre*. The graph *g* reflects a voiceless sound [tš]; cf. the variant *dich*. The collateral development of *ct* to *it* gives us the form *dit* via * *diit*.

meitatz < * *me(d)ietātis*. A reduction of the pretonic diphthong gives the alternate forms *mitat* and *metat*.

sen does not continue CL *sensu*, but is of Germanic origin (< Frankish * *sin*); cf. German *Sinn*. This noun is contained in the verb *forsenar* and Fr. *forcené* from the Old French verb *forsener*, from *fŏris* + * *sin*, quite literally 'to be out of one's mind'. Italian has kept both *senno* and *senso* whereas, in French, *sen* has merged with *sens*.

.us is the enclitic form of *vos*.

sapchatz < *sapiatis*. This four syllable word in Classical Latin suffers syncopation of one syllable in Vulgar Latin through the change of the vowel *i* into a non-syllabic yod. The *p* is kept intact at the end of the first syllable, where it helps determine the voiceless outcome of syllable-initial yod: [tš], spelled *ch*, as opposed to [dž] in absolute initial (cf. *iacēre* > *jazer*; *iam* > *ja*) as well as in various combinations of yod with a voiced sound (cf. CL *rabies* > VL *rabia* > *rauja*; *brĕviāre* > *breujar*). Alternate forms for the treatment of *pi̯* are: *sapiatz*, with retention of the cluster, and *sachatz*, where *p* is completely assimilated into the following [tš] sound. This last development parallels that of French.

el < *ĭlle* is the masc. pronoun of the nom. sing.; it refers back to *vostre sen*. The *el* that follows is a neuter, subject of an impersonal construction (cf. Fr. *il est bien vrai*), and one might have expected a neuter *ver* instead of the masculine form *vers*. This rule, however, is not very strictly enforced in Provençal; cf. *dreitz es que mals l'en aveigna* (Hamlin, 9, 68). Another example of *vers* used as a neuter appears in the *vida* of Peire Vidal: *el crezia que tot fos vers*, where the word it refers to, *tot*, has the proper neuter form. The true domain of neuter adjectives is mostly limited to a few set phrases such as *m'es bel, m'es greu, m'es semblan*; cf. *tan m'es bel quan n'aug ben dire* (Hamlin, 44, 7); *mas grieu er qu'en mar no.l debur* (ib. 13, 16). Yet a few examples were found of neuter adjectives outside of these locutions: *so que a lui era enseignat* (Boutière, p. 188, 32); *so qe li fo dig d'el non era ver* (ib., p. 169, 143-44); and also *saubut fo* 'it was learned'; *fon crezut* 'it was believed'.

E.l reis dis: "*Eu cre ben qu'el vos sia aras faillitz.*" "*Seingner, dis En Bertrans, ben m'es faillitz.*" "*E com?*" *dis lo reis*. 'And the king said: "I am sure that it has failed you now." "Lord, said Bertran, yes, it has failed me, indeed." "And how?" said the king.'

cre ben. The subjunctive is used after *cre ben*, since the addition of *ben* points to a subjective or attenuated belief. The same modal syntax is characteristic of Old French; cf. *tres bien quidat e bien creeit que la beste Bisclavret seit* (Marie de France, *Lais*, *Bisclavret*, v. 273).

cre < *crēdo*. Provençal also has *crei* which draws its -*i* from *vei* (< *vĭdeo*), *ai* (< VL * *aio*), etc. *Crei* is a very common form in the troubadour poetry, and it is recommended by Raimon Vidal who suggests that one should say *ieu crei* just like *ieu vei*. Final *d* is lost in *crēdo* (cf. *crūdu* > *cru*), but other words show a desonorization of *d*: *nūdu* > *nut*.

faillitz. The graph indicates a palatal *l* which is phonological only in combinations with yod. CL *fallĕre* > VL * *fallīre* should give * *falir*, and VL * *fallītus* should go to * *falitz*. A palatal *l* is obtained in *fallio, falliat*, then spreads to the entire verb paradigm: *falhir, falhitz*, etc.; cf. *salīre* > *salhir* and Fr. *saillir*, but Sp. *salir*.

"*Seingner, dis En Bertrans, lo jorn que.l valens Joves rei, vostre fillz, mori, eu perdei lo sen e.l saber e la conoissensa.*" 'Lord, said Bertran, on the day the valorous Young King, your son, died, I lost my judgment and my reason.'

jorn < *diŭrnu*. In certain areas of Romania, the adjective *diŭrnu* is used instead of (or along with) the noun *dies*: Pr. *jorn*, Fr. *jour*, It. *giorno*. Compare the noun *hiems*, which is everywhere replaced by (*tĕmpus*) *hībĕrnum* > Pr. *invern, ivern*, Fr. *hiver*, It. *inverno*, etc. Fifth declension nouns, to which CL *dies* belongs, change into the first declension in -*a* in Vulgar Latin. This change was facilitated by the existence in Latin of collateral forms such as *materies - materia, luxuries - luxuria*. CL *rabies* thus became VL *rabia*, and CL *dies* gave VL *dia*. This noun, *dia*, also survives in Provençal where, true to its fluctuating gender in Classical Latin, it can be either masculine or feminine: *en aquel dia, trastota dia*. The noun is, of course, also continued in the names of the days of the week: *dijous, divenres*, etc.; *di* precedes in Provençal, and the same sequence obtains for the Picard dialect of Northern France (*divenres*), whereas French itself shows the opposite word order: *vendredi*.

valens < * *valentis*. Of the present participle endings of Latin, -*ante*, -*ente* and -*iente*, only two are continued in Provençal where -*iente* is absorbed by -*ente*: *cantante* > *cantan*; *habente* > *aven*; *dīcente* > *dizen*; *part(i)ente* > *parten*. Compare French which generalizes -*ante* (> -*ant*) throughout: *chantant, ayant, disant, partant*. Flexionally is to be observed that the Classical Latin nominative is not continued; *cantans* would give * *cantas*, and *valens* would give * *vales*, etc. The present participles belong to a class of nouns and adjectives that draw their nominative form from an analogy with the accusative: from *valente* comes * *valentis*, in the same way as * *pŏtestātis* (> *podestatz*), based on *pŏtestāte* (> *podestat*), replaces CL *potéstas*, thereby eliminating an imparisyllabic flexion. The gerund is derived from the ablative case: (*in*) *plorando* > *en ploran*, and is consequently invariable.

mori < * *mŏrū(v)it*. Three sets of endings, -*i*, -*it* and -*ic*, exist for the 3. pers. sing. of the perf. ind. of -*ire* verbs: *mori, morit, moric*; *parti, partit, partic*. The norm is -*i*, with -*it* being analogical from perfects in *-et* (*vendet, cantet*) or a mere graphical — poetic licence, while *-ic* is based on the strong perfect formation in *c, g* (*ac, aguist*).

perdei < VL *perdĕdī < CL *pérdĭdī*. The final long *ī* gives rise to optionally diphthongized forms in the 1. and 2. pers. sing. of the perf. ind.: *perdiei* and *perdiest*; these forms are, however, much less frequent than *perdei* and *perdest*.

E.l reis, quant auzi so qu'En Bertrans li dis en ploran, del fil, venc li gran dolors al cor, de pietat, et als oills, si que no.is poc tener qu'el non pasmes de dolor. 'And when the king heard what Bertran tearfully told him about the son, he was stricken with grief in his heart from compassion; he was in tears and could not help fainting from grief.'

venc li granz dolors. The pause that follows *del fil* makes it impossible to begin a new breath group with a weak pronoun *li*; instead, *li* is placed after the verb. A sentence (or an independent portion of a sentence) cannot be introduced by an unstressed pronoun preceding the verb, nor is such a word order normally permitted after the coordinating conjunction *e, et*, although there are exceptions here. There are other examples of this syntax in our excerpt: *referrent li gracias*; *e remanseron ne trei fill*. Compare also this example: *el se crozet e mes se en mar. E pres lo malautia en la nau* (Hamlin, 16, 4-5).

pietat < *piĕtāte*. *Piĕtas - piĕtāte* is treated as a learned word with retention of the hiatus vowel. It is, nevertheless, not totally resistant to change: vowel harmony is evident in *piatat*, and reduction of pretonic *ie* to *i* yields the form *pitat*. Yet, in spite of the fact that it may even evolve to *pidat*, it cannot be considered an entirely popular word.

no.is. This enclitic construction has *.is* for *se*, an alternate form of *.s*.

no.is poc tenre qu'el non pasmes de dolor. Tener, in this common expression of prevention, is always constructed with a negated subordinate clause in the subjunctive in spite of the identity of subject. This same syntax is also characteristic of Old French; cf. *tenir ne me poi qu'adonc Deduit veoir n'alasse* (*Roman de la Rose*, v. 708-709).

pasmes. CL *spasmare* loses its initial *s* through dissimilation to become VL *pasmare* > *pasmar*, Fr. *pâmer*. Otherwise, an initial *sp* would have called for the addition of a prosthetic vowel *e*; cf. *spīna* > *espina*.

E quant el revenc de pasmazon, el crida e dis en ploran: "*En Bertrans, En Bertrans, vos avetz ben drech, et es ben razos, si vos avetz perdut lo sen per mon fill, qu'el vos volia meils que ad home del mon.*" 'And when he returned to his senses, he called out in tears and said: "Bertran, Bertran, you are quite right, and it is only to be expected that you should lose your judgment because of my son, for he loved you more than anybody in the world."'

crida is a perfect tense, an example of the occurrence, in the troubadour biographies, of the 3. pers. sing. of the perfect formation in *-avit* > *-at* > *-a*. The etymology is CL *quiritāvit* > VL * *critāt* > *cridá*, Fr. *cria*.

razos is not a continuation of the Classical Latin nominative case *ratio*, but rather is derived from a Vulgar Latin nominative * *rationis*, if it is not simply drawn from the accusative *razo* to which a flexional *s* has been added. It is difficult to establish the exact chronology of this development. If it dates back to Vulgar Latin, then a postulated * *rationis* is the proper solution, but it may very well have occurred later. This particular problem is, of course, limited to Gallo-Romance, since it is linked with the two-case system.

"*Et eu, per amor de lui, vos quit la persona e l'aver e.l vostre castel e vos ren la mia amor e la mia gracia, e vos don cinc cenz marcs d'argen per los dans que vos avetz receubutz.*" "'And because of my love for him, I will leave you free to dispose of your person, your possessions and your castle, and I readmit you to my friendship and good favor, and I give you 500 marks in silver to make up for the damage you have suffered."'

et < *ĕt* is learned spelling for the standard form *e*, and our text shows no distribution of *et* used before a vowel versus *e* before a consonant; cf. *et l'autre*; *e anet*. In fact, where proclitic *et* allows for intervocalic treatment of the final dental, the result is *ez*, modeled on *ad* > *az* before a vowel: *ab la ploia ez al gel* (Appel: Chr., 10, 16). Regular development would have given * *ed*.

lui is not the only tonic form of the masculine personal pronoun of the 3. pers. sing. where we also find *el* and *elh* used: *ves el*, *per elh*. In the plural, the tonic forms of the masculine are *els*, *elhs* and *lor*: *per els, quascuns d'elhs, senes lor*.

.l vostre castel. Possessives indicating a plurality of owners, *nostre, vostre* and *lor*, do not present any clear-cut formal distinction between the tonic and the unstressed series. The presence or absence of an article, *lo vostre castel* versus *vostre castel*, thus seems to be the only guiding principle in an interpretation of these forms; there is, however, a certain amount of fluctuation in the use of the article with possessives, so that even this criterion seems invalidated.

ren < *rendo*. CL *reddĕre* becomes VL *rendĕre* by analogy with *vendĕre* and VL *prendĕre*.

la mia amor. *Amor* is also feminine in Old French and has remained so in the plural. A rare case of *amor* as a masculine noun was encountered in the troubadour biographies: *per lo vostro amor e per la vostra graçia* (Boutière, p. 277, 40-41).

mia is the tonic form of the feminine possessive adjective. Gallo-Romance requires a closure of CL *mĕa* to * *mēa*, which may have come about through vocalic dissimilation. Old Fr. *meie* and *moie* are clearly derived from a form with a stressed free *ę* (> *ei* > *oi*), and Pr. *mia* is based on the hiatus position of *ę* (cf. *vĭa* > *via*; CL *sĭt* > VL * *sĭat* > *sia*). Besides *mia*, Provençal also has a form *mieua*, analogical from masc. *mieu*. A similar formation in French, a fem. *mienne* drawn from masc. *mien*, completely replaces Old Fr. *meie, moie*. The weak feminine possessives in Provençal are *ma, ta, sa* and, in the plural, *mas, tas, sas*.

gracia, from CL *gratia*, shows learned treatment of the *tį* cluster which, intervocalically, should give a voiced *s*; cf. *ratiōne* > *razó*. Fr. *grâce* is also of a learned nature; cf. Fr. *raison*.

cinc < VL *cīnque* < CL *quīnque*. An early simplification of the initial [*kw*] cluster to *k* through dissimilation explains the subsequent Romance palatalization; cf. Fr. *cinq*, It. *cinque*, Sp. *cinco*. Under normal development, [*kw*] before *e* and *i* is reduced to *k* too late for any participation in the palatalization process: CL *quiētu* > VL *quētu* > Pr. *quet*, Fr. *coi*, Sp. Pg. *quedo*.

dans < *damnos*. Final *mn* usually gives *n*: *damnu* > *dan* and also *dam*; *sŏmnu* > *son* and also *som*. The preference for *n* could come from the plural in view of the dental quality of *s*.

receubutz. CL *receptum* is replaced by an *-ūtu* participle, *recepūtu, which should give *recebut*, a form which, if it has at all existed, was eliminated at an early stage by *receubut*, built on the perfect stem. A variant, *receuput*, attested in the deeds, is borrowed from *receup*; compare the graphs *saub* and *saup* treated above.[60]

En Bertrans si.l cazec als pes, referrent li gracias e merces. E.l reis ab tota la soa ost s'en anet. 'Bertran kneeled down at his feet and thanked him. And the king left with his whole army.'

si.l cazec contains the enclitic form of the dative *li*. *Cazec* is analogical from the strong perfects and alternates with a regular *cazet*.

la soa. *Sŭa* and *tŭa* give the strong possessives *soa* and *toa*. The other strong feminine forms, *sieua* and *tieua*, are drawn from masc. *sieu* and *tieu* and thus form a parallel to the above-mentioned 1. pers. sing. *mieua*. We saw that *mia* is obtained from *mēa because

---

[60] Grafström (Morph., §§ 68 and 69, a) discusses the participial formation in *-ūtu* and lists the participial forms of *recebre*. He gives an example, found in a Quercynois deed, of *receuta* < CL *recepta*; the peculiar development of *pt* in this example parallels that of *ps* to *us* in *ĭpsu* > *eus*, and is encountered also in Portuguese: *præceptu* > Old Pg. *preceuto*.

of the position of ę in hiatus; similarly, *toa* and *soa* can evolve to *tua* and *sua*, and these forms are, indeed, quite common. In the deeds, *sua* is even far more frequent than *soa* and can in no way be considered learned. Grafström suggests that *soa* is an earlier form which a subsequent hiatus-caused change to *sua* has not been able to suppress.[61] It would appear from a simple comparison between *mia* and *soa/sua* that the raising of ę to *i* in hiatus is an earlier, more thorough and far-reaching process than that of ǫ to *u*.

En Bertrans, can saup que.l reis d'Arragon l'avia faita si laida fellonia, fon molt iratz ab lo rei N'Anfos. E si sabia com era vengutz al rei Enric esser soudadiers logaditz e sabia com lo reis d'Arragon era vengutz de paubra generacion de Carlades, d'un castel que a nom Carlat, que es en la seingnoria del comte de Rodes. 'When Bertran learned that King Alfonso of Aragon had committed such a treacherous act against him, he became very angry with him. And he knew how the King of Aragon had come with King Henry as a hired soldier, and how he had come from modest ancestry from Carlades, from a castle which is called Carlat, and which is situated within the domain of the count of Rodez.'

laida is from Frankish * *lait* and is assessed by von Wartburg as a borrowing from French. Provençal has both *lag* and *lait*, variants which recall the treatment of *ct*: *factu* > *fag*, *fait*.[62]

soudadiers < medieval Lat. *soldaderius*. The basic word is *sŏlĭdu* (> *solt*, Fr. *sou*), which has left an impressive progeny of suffixated forms in Romance. Old Fr. *soldee* 'what is worth a *sou*' gives birth to a series of nouns: Old Fr. *soldeier, soldoier, soldeer*, etc. 'soldier hired at a certain wage,' Pr. *soldader* and *soudadier*, Old Sp. *soldadero*. Old Fr. *soudart* is abandoned because of the pejorative meaning attached to the *-ard* suffix (cf. *chauffard, pillard*, etc.); it is replaced by an Italian borrowing, *soldat*, while English has kept Old Fr. *soldier*.[63]

---

[61] Cf. Grafström, § 16, 6, d.
[62] Cf. REW 4858a *lait*.
[63] Cf. FEW, art. *solĭdus*; and REW 8069 *sŏlĭdus*.

logaditz < medieval Lat. *locatīcius* 'hired, employed,' a derivation of *lŏcāre* which also gives Old Fr. *loeis* 'who is employed for wages.'[64]

paubra < VL *paupera* < CL *pauper*. The change of this third declension invariable adjective into the first and second declension category (*bonus - bona*) is attested in the *Appendix Probi*, which carries the following entry: *pauper mulier non paupera mulier*. Another instance of a similar declensional change is contained in this example from the *Glossary of Reichenau*: *pergrandem*: *valde grandum*, and there are numerous other cases of this feature in Provençal: *alegra, avinenta, dolenta, granda, trista*, etc.

Carlades: Le Carladez (Cantal). *Carlat*: Carlat (Cantal).

es > *ĕst* is pronounced with a close vowel *ę*, which sets it apart from the 2. pers. plur. *ęs*, variant of the normal *ętz* < *ĕstis*. Some scholars link the closure to *ę* with a false resolution of enclitic *quę.s* to *qu.ęs*. The loss of the final dental is not phonological either, but seems related to a trend to reserve the *-st* ending for the 2. pers. sing., stemming from its use in the perf. ind.: *perdest, cantest*, etc. An analogy from the perfect changes the 2. pers. sing. of the pres. ind. of *esser*, Lat. *ĕs*, to *est*, following which the 3. pers. sing. is reduced to *es* in an effort to maintain a formal distinction between the 2. and 3. person.

Rodes: Rodez (Aveyron).

E.N Peire de Carlat, qu'era seingner del castel, per valor e per proessa, si pres per moiller la comtessa d'Amillau, qu'era caseguda en eretat, e si n'ac un fil, que fon valens e pros, e conquis lo comtat de Proenssa. 'And Peire de Carlat, who was lord of the castle, and who was a brave and courageous man, married the Countess of Millau, who had inherited, and she gave him a son, full of bravery and prowess, and who conquered the county of Provence.'

proessa < *prodĭtia*. Since *-ĭtia* regularly gives a voiced outcome, *-eza*: *beleza, riqueza*, the double *s* graph is surprising, but no rigid

---

[64] Cf. FEW, art. *lŏcāre*.

distinction between the graphs *s, ss* and *z* is maintained in Provençal. One might also be tempted to explain *proessa* in terms of a possible graphic confusion with the Greek suffix *-ĭssa* which gives *-ęssa*, especially in view of the bewildering picture Old French has to offer for these learned or semi-learned suffixes: *proeise, justise, justice, justesse.*

Amillau: Millau (Aveyron).

caseguda is the past participle of *cazer*, built on the analogical perfect *cazec* for *cazet*. *Cazut*, on the other hand, is based on the root of the present tense. A similarly developed double form of a past participle is *avut - agut* (inf. *av-er*, perf. *ac*).

n' is the elided form of the pronominal adverb *ne* < *ĭnde*.

Proenssa < *Provĭncia*. *V* disappears in connection with a back vowel, even if this vowel precedes. In French, the loss of *v* mostly occurs *before* a back vowel, not *after*, although a few examples are available of this development, such as *ovĭcula* > Fr. *ouaille*. A couple of additional examples will serve to illustrate this difference between North and South: *nŏvĕllu* > Pr. *noel*, Fr. *nouvel*; *prŏbare* > Pr. *proar*, Fr. *prouver*.

Et us sos fils si conquis lo comtat de Barsalona et ac nom Raimons Berrengiers, lo quals conquis lo regisme d'Arragon e fo lo premiers reis que anc fos en Arragon. 'And one of his sons, Raimon Berenguer by name, conquered the county of Barcelona and the kingdom of Aragon, and he became the first king there ever was in Aragon.'

us sos fils. It is quite surprising to find the weak form *sos* used in this syntactic construction instead of the full form *seus, sieus*, as is found in the Old French construction *uns miens nies* and the still used, though somewhat archaic expression, *un mien ami*. Crescini states categorically that the strong form is always preceded by the article (outside of its use as a predicate), and that, on the contrary, the weak form never is. [65] The construction we have here

---

[65] Cf. Crescini, p. 84. It is obvious that he refers specifically to the use of the definite article; no mention is made of the particular construction

represents the norm: *e fetz un so sirventes* (Stimming, 14, 23-24); *e nafreron Artuset malamen, lui et un son compaingnon. Et Artusetz et us sos compaings aucisseron un Juzieu* (Boutière, p. 60, 27-29). Our readings also yielded a similar construction with *doas*, only here the tonic possessive is used: *e remas Aurenga a doas soas fillas* (Hamlin, 32, 27-28). Likewise in the feminine, the strong form appears in a construction with *una*: *et esposet una soa seror celadamens* (Boutière, p. 322, 13-14).

lo quals is a relative pronoun endowed with a full flexion that permits a clear distinction as to number, case and gender: *lo cals* (sing.) - *li cal* (plur.); *li cal* (nom.) - *los cals* (acc.); *los cals* (masc.) - *las cals* (fem.) - *lo cal* (neuter), etc. This pronoun can thus help alleviate any confusion that might result from a marked trend in Provençal towards the indiscriminate use of *que* for all genders and in all syntactic functions.

regisme < *rĕgĭmen*. The continuation of Lat. *ĭ* as *i* is a learned feature; cf. Fr. *régime*. Provençal does have forms with *e*: *regesme, regeme*; the unetymological *s* may come from the suffix -*ĭsmu*. The word *rĕgĭmen* suffered an early contamination by *regale*, leading to the creation of a hypothetic *regálimen* which gives Pr. Old Fr. *reialme* and *realme*, Fr. *royaume*. Engl. *realm* is borrowed from Gallo-Romance.[66]

premiers < VL *prīmarius* < CL *prīmus*; cf. *primver* < *prīmu vēru*, and compare Fr. *printemps* < *prīmu tĕmpus*. Continuations of CL *prīmus* seem to be more common in Provençal than in French, whether with the original meaning of 'first': *de la ora nona*

---

with the indefinite article. But even granted this limitation, his statement is too categorical, since exceptions *do* occur, if only as mere poetic licences; cf. *mas quar trop lens tornei en sai, on seus bels cors sojorn' e jai* (Peire Vidal, XXIX, 13-15, in J. Anglade: *les Poésies de Peire Vidal*, Paris, 1923). Compare also this example, from Boutière, p. 14, 6-7: *e pres una maniera de trobar en caras rimas, per que soas cansons no son leus ad entendre*. *Soa domna* is found alternating quite frequently with *la soa domna*, an interesting parallel with Italian syntax where the possessive takes no article when used about certain family relationships. The difficulty of establishing a clear division in the old deeds between tonic and weak possessives is outlined by Grafström: Morph., § 26.

[66] Cf. FEW, art. *regimen*; and REW 7170 *rĕgĭmen*.

del dissapte entro la prima del dilus (Appel: Chr., 117, 78-79), or with various figurative connotations such as 'excellent, clever, fine, tender': *totz hom prims* 'every intelligent man' (ib., 123, 10); *lo cuer ac blanc e prim e tenre* (ib., 4, 162). Furthermore, the word survives in a series of adverbial constructions: *primas, de prima(s), al prim* 'at the beginning, from the beginning.' The phonological development of *prīmarius* to *premiers* shows labialization or rounding of pretonic *ī* to [ə], caused by the following *m*. This labialization process may also lead to a change to [y]: *prumier*; *hībĕrnu* > *uvern*.

anc < *anque, which is of unknown origin. It means 'ever' or 'never,' is usually accompanied by a negation when of a negative meaning: *anc non agui de me poder,* and may even be reinforced by *mai*: *et eu non o saubi anc mai*. Rohlfs relates *anc* to the adverb *ancar*, It. *ancora*, Fr. *encore*.[67]

lo premiers reis que anc fos. The subjunctive, when used following a superlative, serves to put forth an attenuated or subjective rather than a categorical statement. A few equivalents of a superlative (*lo sols, lo premiers*) may also be constructed with a subjunctive in spite of the factual and precise nature of a word like *lo premiers*. It is followed by an indicative in this example, from Boutière, p. 218, 4-5: *e fo lo premiers bons trobaire que fon outra mon*.

E anet penre corona a Roma; e, cant s'en tornava e fon al borc Saint Dalmas, el mori. E remanseron ne trei fill: Anfos, lo quals fo reis d'Arragon, aquest que fetz lo mal d'En Bertran de Born, e l'autre, don Sancho, et l'autre, Berrengiers de Besaudunes. 'He went to receive his crown in Rome; and on the way back, when he was at the town of San Dalmazio, he died. He left behind three sons: Alfonso, who was King of Aragon, the one who betrayed Bertran de Born; don Sancho and Berenguer de Besalú.'

---

[67] Cf. Rohlfs, p. 74; FEW, art. *anque*; and REW 488 *anque. Old French has *ainc* 'never', Italian has *anche* 'also'. Von Wartburg maintains that *anque is totally lacking on the Iberian Peninsula, yet Meyer-Lübke quotes an Asturian-Galician *anque*.

penre < VL *prendĕre* < CL *prehendĕre*. The phonological outcome of VL *prendĕre* is *prendre*, which contains a sequence of *r - r*, susceptible of a dissimilation whereby the first *r* is eliminated: *prendre* > *pendre*, a form which is well attested. A similar change may be observed in: *granré* > *ganré*; *prestre* > *pestre*. The subsequent change of *pendre* to *penre* is difficult to account for. It could reflect the alternance between *nr* and *ndr*, the insertion of a *d* into the *n'r* cluster being entirely optional: *ponĕre* > *ponre* and *pondre*; *honorare* > *onrar* and *ondrar*.⁶⁸

borc < *bŭrgu*, a word of Germanic origin which also survives in Fr. *bourg* and It. *borgo*. The adjective *borges* 'who belongs to a *burgu*' is formed by adding the suffix *-ense*; cf. Lat. *Atheniense*.

Saint Dalmas: San Dalmazio (near Genoa).

remanseron < *remansĕrunt*. The Classical Latin stressed ending of the 3. pers. plur. of the perf. ind., *-ērunt*, is not continued in Vulgar Latin which substitutes an unstressed *-ĕrunt* for it: *hábuĕrunt* > *ágron*; *sápuĕrunt* > *saupron*; *vídĕrunt* > *viron*. The stressed *-éron* ending is borrowed from the weak *dĕdī* perfect: *vendęron, cantęron*, and is often found alternating with regular strong perfects: *agron* and *agueron* (< *habuĕrunt*); *preiron* and *prezeron* (< *pre(h)ensĕrunt*); *remairon* (*remazon*) and *remazeron* (< *remansĕrunt*). The retention of *n* before *s* is analogically determined through influence of the infinitive *remaner*; a phonological *remaseron* is actually more common than *remanseron*. Compare the analogical retention of *ns* in Fr. *défense* because of *défendre*.

ne < *ĭnde*, a proclitic word which may also be reduced to *en*. The pronominal function of *ne* and *en* corresponds to that of Fr. *en*.

---

⁶⁸ See Grafström: Morph., § 48, b, who proposes a homonymic clash with *pendre* < *pendĕre* as a possible reason for the change. He goes on to suggest an analogy with *pren* < *prendo*, where the reduction of final- *nd* to *n* is normal. However, the 1. pers. sing. of the pres. ind. is totally isolated in the paradigm, and it would therefore seem far more plausible for an analogy to work in the opposite direction (cf. *mand* for *man* < *mando*, based on *mandar, mandam, mandatz*, etc.).

trei is a nominative drawn from *tres* < *trēs*. The *-s* which, in masculine nouns, signals an acc. plur., is dropped, and the new nominative, *trei* (not *tre*), is modeled on VL *dŭī*.

aquest < *accu-ĭste. The reinforcement of *ĭste* is made with *eccu* + *ac* or *atque*. The secondary [kw], which arises from this combination, is simplified to *k*, but is not assibilated.

don Sancho. The apocopated form *don* from *domĭne* is not commonly used as a title in Provençal where *domĭne* is continued in the far more indigenous form *En*. *Don* appears here with a Spanish name, but compare *lo rei N'Anfos*. One example was encountered of *don* used as a direct address form: *don, oc* 'yes, Sir' (Appel: Chr., 64, 78). In the deeds, it functions as a title implying distinction or merit: *don Girau de Murs* (Brunel, 36,6); *e Guio le donz* (ib., 459,4). Its exact value escapes us, but Brunel is inclined to equate it with *monseigneur*.

E saup com el avia traïda la filla de l'emperador Manuel, que l'emperaire l'avia mandada per moiller ab grant tresor et ab grant aver et ab molt honrada compaingnia, e los raubet de tot l'aver que la domna e.ill Grec avian. 'And he (Bertran) knew how he (Alfonso) had betrayed the daughter of the emperor Manuel, the emperor having sent him his daughter to marry, with great treasures and large sums of money and very distinguished company, and he robbed them of all the money the lady and the Greeks had with them.'

traïda < *tradīta, with a change in conjugation from *tradĕre* to *tradīre. There are numerous other cases of the loss of intervocalic *d* instead of the regular change to a voiced *s*: *cōda* > *coa*; *sūdōre* > *suor* and *suzor*; CL *praeda* > *prēda > *prẹa* and *prẹza*.

tresor is a French borrowing; the regular Provençal development is *thesauru* > *tezaur*, with retention of the diphthong *au* and without the addition of an unetymological *r*.

raubet is the perfect of *raubar*, from Germanic *raubôn, a relatively recent loan in which *b* has not undergone its normal change to *v* in intervocalic position, as in *habētis* > *avetz*; *faba*

> *fava*. Germanic *b* is also kept in It. *rubare, roba*, and in Fr. *dérober, robe*; compare *dēbēre* > It. *dovere*, Fr. *devoir*.

.ill. The enclitic form of the masc. plur. article in the nominative case, *li*, is *.ill, .lh* or *.il*, all different graphs for the same sound, a palatal *l*: *et li* > *e.ill, e.lh, e.il*.

Grec < *Graecī*. *Graecu* and *Graecī* both give *Grec*; the final -*ī* of the nom. plur. does not normally exert any influence on the preceding consonant nor on the stem-vowel, since this would create an asymmetric plural formation. Its influence seems limited to a few cases of palatalization of *l* and *t*: *capellī* > *cabelh*; *nūllī* > *nulh*; *amātī* > *amag, amach*, and these are only sporadical occurrences. In a unique case of a nom. plur., final -*ī* affects both the vowel (through *umlaut*) and the final stem consonant: CL *tōtī* > VL *tōttī* (a case of expressive gemination) > *tutti > *tuch, tug*.[69]

e com los enviet per mar, marritz e consiros e desconseillatz, e com sos fraire Sanchos l'avia touta Proenssa, e com s'esperjuret, per l'aver que.l reis Enrics li det, contra.l comte de Tolosa. 'And (he knew) how he had sent them away by sea, sad, worried and confused, and how his brother Sancho had taken Provence away from him, and how he was guilty of perjury (because of the money King Henry had given him) against the count of Toulouse.'

---

[69] See A. Thomas: "Le Nominatif Pluriel asymétrique des Substantifs masculins en ancien provençal," in *Romania*, vol. 34, p. 353. For Old Fr. *tuit* < * *tutti* < *tōtti*, see Rheinfelder, § 237; and Fouché, vol. 2, p. 398. Fouché suggests an explanation based on syntactic phonetics: *tutti omini* > *tuttj omini*, with the *i* transformed into a yod before a noun beginning with a vowel. See also Rohlfs (p. 163) who terms the development of *tōttī* to Pr. Old Fr. *tuit* "eine eigenartige Entwicklung, die durch keine genaue französische Parallele sich stützen lässt," and who finds the Provençal form *tuch*, collateral form of *tuit*, "noch eigenartiger." Certain Northern Italian dialects possess an asymmetric plural formation for masculine nouns which have *a* as a stem vowel in the singular and inflect this *a* to *e* in the plural under the influence of final -*ī*. At Santa-Maria-Maggiore, we find: *rat - rèt*; *gat - ghèt*; *kamp - kèmp*; at Barbania: *traf - trèf*; at Quarna (Novara); *balm - bèlm*, etc. For additional examples, consult G. Bertoni: *Italia dialettale*, Milano, 1916, p. 61. Regular phonological evolution has thus made havoc of the declension system by substituting a vocalic alternance for flexional endings.

enviet, the perfect of *enviar* < *ĭn-vĭāre*, shows raising of *e* to *i* in hiatus; cf. Old Fr. *enveer*, and compare Pr. *via* with Fr. *voie* < *vĭa*.

marritz is derived from the Frankish verb * *marrjan* > *marrir*; the adjective *marri* is extremely common in Old French, but is now archaic or literary.

consiros or *cossiros* represents a combination of the verb *consirar* and the suffix *-ōsus*. *Consīd(e)rāre* > *consirar*; the *d'r* cluster is resolved in a yod + *r*, but the yod is absorbed by the preceding vowel *ī*.

touta < *tollĭta* agrees grammatically with *Proenssa*, even though it precedes the direct object. Agreement with the direct object, whether it precedes or follows, seems to be the norm: *quan Richartz ac facha la patz* (Stimming, 24, 1); *quar avian la patz facha* (ib., 17, 62); but there are infrequent cases of non-agreement as well, when the direct object follows: *en Bertrans avia escriut en son cor totz los mals* (ib., 24, 11-12).

Proenssa. Names of countries, provinces, districts are not accompanied by any article; cf. *ma provision pour Bretagne* (Madame de Sévigné).

s'esperjuret. *Perjurar* is here reinforced by the prefix *ex-*; cf. *esgardar* < *ex-* + * *wardon*; *esdevenir, escombatre*, etc.

det < *dĕdit* is the 3. pers. sing. of the perf. ind. The *-it* ending is dropped, and *d* is desonorized in final position. The pre-desonorization stage can be observed in the *Sainte Foi d'Agen*, which has *ded*. The *-et* ending of the weak perfects (*vendet, cantet*) is analogical from *det*, which plays an important role in their very formation; cf. *pérdĭdit* > * *perdĕdit* > *perdet* and the subsequent extension of this perfect type into the *e* and *a* conjugations.

E de totas aquestas razons fetz En Bertrans de Born lo sirventes que ditz: Pois lo gens terminis floris. 'And from all these motifs Bertran de Born composed the *sirventes* which begins: Since the delightful flower season.'

Pois lo gens terminis floris. This *sirventes,* written in 1184, lashes out against Alfonso II of Aragon, an ally of King Henry II of England in his battles to gain control over Provence. Even with all its historical inaccuracies, the extended *razó* that leads up to this poem serves the purpose of guiding the reader to a better understanding of the events related in the *sirventes.* The need for an explanatory *razó* is here closely tied up with the very nature of the *sirventes,* a satirical poetic genre which draws its inspiration from the events of the day. With the lapse of time, events of even the greatest magnitude tend to fade from the memory, and poems dealing with such fleeting subject matter will soon require an extensive commentary in order to be understood and appreciated. The invocation of Spring at the beginning of the poem is a purely conventional theme that recurs over and over again in the troubadour poetry. A few examples, all quoted from the opening lines of poems, will serve as an illustration of this traditional motif: *Ab la dolchor del temps novel* (Guilhem de Peitieus); *Can l'erba fresch' e.lh folha par* (Bernart de Ventadorn); *Can lo glatz e.l frechs e la neus s'en vai* (Giraut de Bornelh). An amusing satire of this procedure is found in a poem by Cercamon: *Puois nostre temps comens' a brunezir.* The *sirventes, Pois lo gens terminis floris,* can be found in Hamlin's *Introduction à l'Étude de l'Ancien Provençal* as well as in Stimming's *Bertran von Born.*

THE TROUBADOUR POETRY

The classical and literary language of Southern France appeared towards the end of the 11th century and flourished for a couple of centuries as the most harmonious and perfect of the Romance tongues. It was cultivated at the courts of Southern France, from where its fame was carried to Italy and Spain by the wandering troubadours. The sudden appearance on the European stage of Provençal poetry, its immediate achievement of perfection, its conventional theme of courtly love, its important role as the point of departure for European lyrical poetry, all of these are questions, among many others, that cannot be taken up in a linguistically oriented work.[70]

The number of troubadour poets is truly astounding; the Pillet — Carstens bibliography lists approximately 460 names of troubadours whose work has been at least partially preserved. These poets were recruited from all classes of society: rich and powerful noblemen (Guilhem de Peitieus, Jaufré Rudel, Bertran de Born, Raimbaut d'Aurenga), humble knights (Sordel, Cadenet, Peirol), bishops (Folquet de Marseilla) and other members of the clergy

---

[70] Numerous works are available in the field of Old Provençal literature: besides the already quoted works by A. Jeanroy and Martín de Riquer, one may consult J. Anglade: *les Troubadours*, Paris: Colin, 1929; P. Rémy: *la Littérature provençale au Moyen Age*, Bruxelles, 1944; E. Hoepffner: *les Troubadours*, Paris: Colin, 1955, just to mention a few. For bibliographical works on the troubadour poetry, see A. Pillet and H. Carstens: *Bibliographie des Troubadours*, Halle: Niemeyer, 1933; and valuable bibliographical material is found in G. Rohlfs: *Romanische Philologie*, Heidelberg, 1950-52; C. Tagliavini: *Le Origini delle Lingue neolatine*, Bologna: Pàtron, 1964; and the already mentioned work by F. Hamlin.

(Gausbert de Poicibot, Peire Cardenal, the monk of Montaudon), judges (Lanfranc Cigala), the rich bourgeois class (Peire d'Alvernhe) and ordinary merchants or workers (Peire Vidal, son of a furrier; Bernart de Ventadorn, son of a servant; Giraut de Bornelh, *hom de bas afar*). It is safe to say lyrical poetry has never since been able to regain the same firm grip over the life of a whole society.

The composition of a couple of grammatical treatises on the language of the troubadours, the *Razos de Trobar* by Raimon Vidal de Besalú and the *Donatz proensals* by Uc Faidit, both of which are from the 13th century, bears further witness to the great prestige of Provençal, considered almost on a par with the classical languages of Antiquity, centuries before Spanish or French could command the same respect.

Three poems, quoted *in extenso*, are offered here as samples of the troubadour poetry. Our selection comprises a famous *cansó* by Bernart de Ventadorn, *Can vei la lauzeta mover*, known as the *Chanson de l'Alouette*; a poem by a very talented *trobairitz*, the Countess of Dia, who laments her lover's faithlessness, *A chantar m'er de so q'ieu no volria*; and Giraut de Bornelh's beautiful *alba*: *Reis glorios, verais lums e clartatz*, a poem which describes the parting at dawn of lovers, warned of imminent dangers by the *gaita*.

1. BERNART DE VENTADORN: Can vei la lauzeta mover.

    I. Can vei la lauzeta mover
        de joi sas alas contra.l rai,
        que s'oblid' e.s laissa chazer
        per la doussor c'al cor li vai,
5   ai! tan grans enveya m'en ve
        de cui qu'eu veya jauzion,
        meravilhas ai, car desse
        lo cor de dezirer no.m fon.

    II. Ai, las! tan cuidava saber
10   d'amor, e tan petit en sai!
        Car eu d'amar no.m posc tener
        celeis don ja pro non aurai.
        Tout m'a mo cor, e tout m'a me,
        e se mezeis e tot lo mon;
15   e can se.m tolc, no.m laisset re
        mas dezirer e cor volon.

    III. Anc non agui de me poder
        ni no fui meus de l'or en sai
        que.m laisset en sos olhs vezer
20   en un miralh que mout me plai.
        Miralhs, pus me mirei en te,
        m'an mort li sospir de preon,
        c'aissi.m perdei com perdet se
        lo bels Narcisus en la fon.

25   IV. De las domnas me dezesper;
        ja mais en lor no.m fiarai;

c'aissi com las solh chaptener,
enaissi las deschaptenrai.
Pois vei c'una pro no m'en te
vas leis que.m destrui e.m cofon,
totas las dopt' e las mescre,
car be sai c'atretals se son.

V. D'aisso.s fa be femna parer
ma domna, per qu'e.lh o retrai,
car no vol so c'om deu voler,
e so c'om li deveda, fai.
Chazutz sui en mala merce,
et ai be faih co.l fols en pon;
e no sai per que m'esdeve,
mas car trop puyei contra mon.

VI. Merces es perduda, per ver,
(et eu non o saubi anc mai),
car cilh qui plus en degr' aver,
no.n a ges, et on la querrai?
A! can mal sembla, qui la ve,
qued aquest chaitiu deziron
que ja ses leis non aura be,
laisse morir, que no l'aon!

VII. Pus ab midons no.m pot valer
precs ni merces ni.l dreihz qu'eu ai,
ni a leis no ven a plazer
qu'eu l'am, ja mais no.lh o dirai.
Aissi.m part de leis e.m recre;
mort m'a, e per mort li respon,
e vau m'en, pus ilh no.m rete,
chaitius, en issilh, no sai on.

VIII. Tristans, ges no.n auretz de me,
qu'eu m'en vau, chaitius, no sai on.
De chantar me gic e.m recre,
e de joi e d'amor m'escon.

Can vei la lauzeta mover de joi sas alas contra.l rai, que s'oblid' e.s laissa chazer per la doussor c'al cor li vai, 'When I see the lark flap its wings with joy against the ray of sunlight, faint and let itself fall to the ground because of the sweetness that penetrates its heart.'

vei < *vĭdeo*. When final, *dį* is simplified to *į*: *radiu* > *rai*; *pŏdiu* > *poi*. Or else, the result is [*tš*], rarely [*ts*]; the graphs are varied (*ch, g, h, tz*): *gaudiu* > *gaug, gauch*; *ĭnŏdiu* > *enueg, enueitz*; *audio* > *aug, auch*; *pŏdiu* > *Poh* (proper name attested in the old deeds).

lauzeta comes from Gaulish *alauda* to which a diminutive ending *-ĭtta* has been added: (*a*)*laud*(*a*)*-ĭtta* > *lauzeta*. Initial *a* is lost by aphaeresis, probably by deglutination of what was erroneously considered to be part of the article: *l'alauda* > *la lauda*; cf. *l'alegresa* > *la legresa*. The Latin diphthong *au* is kept in Provençal: *gaudiu* > *gaug*; *paucu* > *pauc*.[71] The diminutive suffix *-ĭtta* shows the normal simplification of a geminate: *-tt-* > *t*.

mover < *mŏvĕre*. VL * *mŏvĕre*, obtained through a change in conjugation, is continued as *moure*, with a vocalization of *v* in the secondary *v'r* cluster; cf. *vīvĕre* > *viure*. CL *mŏvēre* gives Fr. *mouvoir*, while It. *muovere* follows from * *mŏvĕre*.

joi, from Lat. *gaudiu*, is a French borrowing, which accounts for the development of *au* to *o*, the regular Provençal outcome being *gaug, gauch*. It is puzzling why the word *joi*, which plays such an important role in troubadour poetry, should have a Northern form.[72] Morphologically, masc. *joi* goes back to a neuter sing. *gaudium*, while the neuter plur. is continued as a fem. sing. in French: *joie* < *gaudia*.

---

[71] Cf. Lausberg, § 243. The retention of *au* is a distinctive feature of Provençal vocalism which Catalan does not share: Cat. *or, poc, goig* < *auru, paucu, gaudiu*; see Badía Margarit, § 47, IV, A. For the fate of *au* in Vulgar Latin, see Väänänen, § 60.

[72] For the role and meaning of *joi* in troubadour poetry, see Riquer (pps. XX-XXXI) who describes in detail the qualities that were required of a perfect lover: *cortezia, joi, solatz, largueza, mezura, joven, ensenhamen*. An exact translation of these terms is often impossible.

oblid' < VL *oblītat*. CL *obliviscor, oblitus sum* was replaced, in Vulgar Latin, by *oblitare*, drawn from the past participle *oblitus*. This procedure is quite common with Classical Latin deponent verbs; compare CL *audeor, ausus sum* > VL *ausare* > *auzar*.

doussor is not derived directly from medieval Lat. *dŭlcōre*, but shows influence of the adjective *dous*, insofar as a velar *c* does not assibilate. Lat *dŭlcis* is invariable as to gender, but is not treated as such in Gallo-Romance where a separate feminine form: Pr. *dolza, dousa*; Fr. *douce*, is encountered from the beginning (the *Boeci* has *dolza ment*), based on a very early change of *dŭlcis* to * *dŭlcius* - * *dŭlcia*.

vai does not go back to *vadit* which develops phonologically to *va* with an early loss of *-it* as well as of *d* in a secondary final position. *Vai* is analogical from *fai* which, itself, is not etymological either, since *facit* should give * *fatz* (cf. *placet* > *platz*). Crescini draws *fai* from an analogy with *traire - trai*, combined with a conscious effort to avoid confusion between *facio* and *facit* which both would merge in *fatz*. [73]

ai! tan grans enveya m'en ve de cui qu'eu veya jauzion, meravilhas ai, car desse lo cor de dezirer no.m fon. 'Alas, I become so jealous of all those I see rejoicing that I am astonished that my heart does not immediately faint with desire.'

grans is a fem. nom. The flexion of third declension adjectives is *granz - grant* in the singular whereas, in the plural, masculine has *grant - granz*, feminine only one form *granz*. Old French follows the same pattern, with an optional *-s* in the nom. case of the fem. sing.

enveya < *ĭnvĭdia*. Corresponding to the voiceless results of *dį* in a final position ([tš] and sometimes [ts]), intervocalic *dį* gives [dž], rarely [dz]; a simplification to *į* may occur in both cases. It is

---

[73] See Crescini, p. 111, for a discussion of *fai* and for the problem of such 3. pers. sing. variants as *platz - plai*; *jatz - jai*; *dutz - dui*.

not clear whether the graph *y* stands for yod or [dž]. Another example of intervocalic *di̯* is *veya* < *vĭdeam*.

ve < *vĕnit*, with an unstable *n* after the early loss of *-it*.

cui is used after a preposition and as an emphatic accusative as well as in a dative-genitive function; its syntax is thus parallel to that of Old Fr. *cui*. The indefinite relative construction, which we have an example of here, is obtained by adding an indefinite *que* to the relative pronoun; the mood is the subjunctive.

eu < VL *eo* < CL *ĕgo*. Following the stressed vowel *e*, final *o* becomes part of the diphthong *eu*, and this secondary *-u* may cause diphthongization of *ĕ*: *ieu*.

jauzion. The verb *gaudēre* gives It. *godere* and, with a change to * *gaudīre*, Pr. *jauzir, gauzir* and Fr. *jouir*. *Jauzion* is derived from this verb with the ending *-on* stemming from the gerund *-ŭndu* (cf. v. 46 *deziron*).

meravilhas is not drawn from CL *mīrabĭlia*, since pretonic *ĭ* would remain, but rather from a Vulgar Latin form in *e* (cf. Fr. *merveille* and It. *meraviglia*). *Meravilha* and a collateral form *meravelha* could represent dialectal differences, based on the action or inaction of palatalized *l* which, in some areas of Romania, will raise *e* to *i*; compare It. *meraviglia* and Ven. *meravegia*.

ai < VL * *aio* < CL *habeo*.

desse represents a combination of *de* + *sem(per)* as proved by the collateral forms *dese* and *desempre*, *ancse* and *ancsempre*. This etymology was already established by Diez, viewed with suspicion by Meyer-Lübke who found it difficult to accept the abbreviation of *semper*, contested by A. Thomas who proposed *semel* as the basis for *se(n)*, but accepted by P. Meyer and, more recently, by von Wartburg. Lewent suggests as etymology the reflexive pronoun *se* without paying much heed to the phonological and semantic difficulties involved, specifically the *-n* of the oldest form, *ancsen*, which appears in the *Sainte Foi d'Agen* (v. 106), and laborious semantic changes, ranging from 'of oneself' via 'voluntarily' to 'easily' and 'immediately'. [74]

dezirer is a noun, based on the root *dezir-* + a suffix which can be either *-er* or *-ier*: *dezirer* and *dezirier*. Similar derivations are encountered in the following lines: *vos est mos gaugs, mos alegriers, e vos est totz mos consirers* (Appel: Chr., 3, 631-632). The infinitive *dezirar* is regularly developed from *desīdĕrare*, with *d'r* going to yod + *r* and the yod then being absorbed by *i*.

fon < *fŭndit*, wiht a stable *n* resulting from the final cluster of *n* + dental.

Ai, las! tan cuidava saber d'amor, e tan petit en sai! Car eu d'amar no.m posc tener celeis don ja pro non aurai. 'Alas, I thought I knew so much about love, yet I know so little about it. For I cannot help but love the woman from whom I shall obtain no favors.'

cuidava. CL *cōgĭtāre* > VL * *cūgĭtāre* > *cuidar*, with the change of *g* to yod and a late syncopation which allows for a voicing of *t* to *d*. The closure of *ǫ* to *u* is caused by the palatal, just like CL *ōstiu* becomes VL * *ūstiu* > *uis, us*; Fr. *huis*.

petit is formed on the root *pitt-*; *pisinnus* and *pitinnus* are attested in inscriptions as seen from the following examples, quoted from G. Rohlfs: *Sermo Vulgaris Latinus*, Halle, Niemeyer, 1951: *hic positus est Argutio pitinnus* (I, 64); *pisinna Victoria* (I, 63).

sai is analogical from *ai* < * *aio* < *habeo*.

posc does not continue *possum* of Classical Latin, but is modeled on *conosc* < *co(g)nosco*.

celeis and *celei* were created with *leis* and *lei* as models.

pro is not attested for Classical Latin, but is drawn from CL *prodest* which, in Vulgar Latin, had become *prode est*. It is this word we find in *prodome, prozome* as well as in Fr. *prud'homme*.

---

[74] Cf. FEW, art. *sĕmper*; and REW 7814 *sĕmper*. The deeds show *per jassempre* alternating with *per jasse*, and they also contain one further example of a form ending in *-sen*: *a jassen*.

aurai comes from the Romance future formation * *habere aio*; the change of *b* to *u̯* is obscure in French (cf. Old Fr. *avrai* as opposed to Fr. *aurai*), but common in Provençal with *b'r*: *scrībĕre* > *escriure*; *lībĕrare* > *liurar*.

Tout m'a mo cor, e tout m'a me, e se mezeis e tot lo mon: e can se.m tolc, no.m laisset re mas dezirer e cor volon. 'She has stolen my heart away, and she has stolen me and herself and everybody; and when she abandoned me, she did not leave me anything but desire and a languishing heart.'

tout < *tŏllĭtu*. VL *tŏllĭtu* replaces CL *sublātu* which is morphologically far removed from the verbal stem and therefore in a weak position where its relationship with *tollĕre* had ceased to be clearly perceived. This is evident in the frequent glosses of this participle in the *Glossary of Reichenau*: *sublata - subportata*; *sublati - tulti*, etc. Vulgar Latin had created both *tŏllĭtu* and *tŭltu* in replacement of CL *sublātum*, both of which could phonologically give Pr. Old Fr. *tout*. Provençal also has a form, *tolgut*, built on the perfect stem.

me is here used as a tonic form; there is no formal distinction between the tonic and the weak form of this pronoun.

mezeis. The etymology is *ĭpsu* reinforced by *met*; cf. *ego* and *egomet*. *Met-ĭpsu* > *medeis*, with *t* voicing to *d*. Appel mentions that this process can sometimes move one step further, i. e. from *d* to *z*, yielding the most common form here, which is *mezeis*. The old deeds show yet another form: *meteis*, for which Grafström proposes the etymology * *mett-ĭpsu*. In the same fashion, *mezeis* could be derived from a postulated * *med-ĭpsu*, obtained through an early voicing. Grandgent attributes *z* to analogical influence of *az, ez, quez* (< *ad, et, quĭd* + *vowel*).[75] The change of *ĭpsu* to *eis* reveals a confusion between *ps* and *cs* (cf. Cat. *eix*), as evidenced also by: *capsa* > *caissa*, Pg. *caixa*, Sp. *caja* (but Fr. *châsse*).[76]

---

[75] Cf. Grafström: Morph., § 31; Appel, § 46b'; and Grandgent, § 65.

[76] Cf. Lausberg, § 429; and Williams, § 85, 3, A. Grafström (Morph., § 34) discusses the triple outcome of *ĭpsu* in the deeds: *eis, eus* and *es* (with *eps* as an older variant of *es*), showing vocalization of *p* to either *i̯* or *u̯* or

tolc < *tŏlluit is the 3. pers. sing. of the perf. ind.

volon for *volen* (< *vŏlente*) is most likely influenced by *-ŭndu*; cf. *jauzion, deziron*, but a fluctuation between *o* and *e* is also evident in *volontat* and *volentat* (< *vŏlŭntāte*); *volontier* and *volentier* (< *vŏlŭntarie*).

Anc non agui de me poder ni no fui meus de l'or en sai que.m laisset en sos olhs vezer en un miralh que mout me plai. 'I no longer had any control over myself nor was I quite myself from the moment when she let me look into her eyes in a mirror that pleases me very much.'

agui is a weak form of the perfect in the 1. pers. sing. The normal development is *habui* > *ac*; *agui* is modeled on weak perfects in *-i*: *sofri, mori, legi*, etc. A collateral form *aic* is difficult to explain, since there is not normally any release of *i* in the stem; it may have been influenced by the pres. ind. *ai*.

fui meus. When functioning as a predicate, the strong possessives are not normally accompanied by any article.

olhs < *ŏculos*. We also have *uelhs* with the optional diphthongization the palatal may cause.

miralh and Old Fr. *mirail* are derived from the verb *mīrāre* 'to look' + the suffix *-(a)culu*.

Miralhs, pus me mirei en te, m'an mort li sospir de preon, c'aissi.m perdei com perdet se lo bels Narcisus en la fon. 'Mirror, ever since I saw my own image reflected in you, deep sighs have killed me, for I lost myself as did the beautiful Narcissus in the fountain.'

miralhs is a nominative used in vocative function.

pus. Pŏst had become *pos* because of its proclitic usage, losing the final *t* before a word beginning with a consonant. A trend

---

reduction of *ps* to *s*. This whole problem has been treated in detail by M. Pfister: *-PS- in den romanischen Sprachen*, Berne, 1960.

towards closing *o* to *u* in pretonic position is widespread in Romania, and this same trend will, of course, also affect proclitic words: *com* and *cum*, *lor* and *lur*. [77]

mort. *Morir* is common as a transitive verb 'to kill'.

preon < *profŭndu*. The change of *o* to *e* may have come about through the substitution of the prefix *prae-* for *pro-*; a raising in hiatus can then give us *prion*, collateral form of *preon*. Another solution is offered by Schultz-Gora who explains the change to *preon* in terms of a vocalic dissimilation, just like *sŭbmŏnĕre* > Old Fr. *semondre*; *rŏtŭndu* > Sp. *redondo*. F is not normally intervocalic in Latin; following a prefix, it is usually treated as initial (cf. *defĕndĕre* > *defendre*; *profĕctu* > *profech*, Fr. *profit*), unless the notion of a composition is lost as in the case of *preon* where the treatment of *f* parallels that of *b* and *v*, which drop before a back vowel.

aissi < *ac sīc*. Provençal also has a combination of *in* + *ac* + *sīc* > *enaissi*; compare *in sīc* > Old Fr. *ensi*; *ac sīc* > Old Fr. *aissi*; and Fr. *ainsi* which, supposedly, results from a combination of the two.

fon < *fŏnte*, and has a stable *n*.

De las domnas me dezesper; ja mais en lor no.m fiarai; c'aissi com las solh chaptener, enaissi las deschaptenrai. 'I despair of the ladies; I shall never again have confidence in them; for as much as I used to protect them, so much more shall I abandon them from now on.'

domnas < *dŏmĭnas*. The *m'n* cluster is either kept or assimilated to *n*: *domna* or *dona*; *fēmĭna* > *femna* or *fenna*. Compare French which has an assimilation to *m*: *dame*, *femme*. Quite frequently,

---

[77] Appel (§§ 33a and 34) derives *pus* from a form with yod: * *pŏstį* > *pueis* (cf. * *pŏstius* > Fr. *puis*) with subsequent reductions to *pues* and *pus*. A VL * *pŏstius* is modeled on *prius*, *mĕlius*, and this same analogy leads to the creation of VL * *antius* from CL *antea*, giving Pr. *anz* and Old Fr. *ainz*.

dompna is encountered, a form which seems to contain nothing more than an arbitrary spelling, although Appel offers a physiological explanation of the *p* as being the result of an "energischen Lippenschluss." It might be the result of a denasalization, creating an implosive *n* and a more distinct syllabic boundary. [78]

lor originates from a genitive plural, *illōrum*; it is used here as a strong form, being the equivalent of *elas* and *elhas*. The Latin feminine form, *illārum*, is not continued.

fiarai. Popular Latin derives *fīdāre from *fīdus* 'faithful'; Italian has *fidare*, and the regular outcome in Provençal is *fizar*. *Fiar* is yet another example of the fluctuation in the treatment of intervocalic *d*; compare *crūdēle* > *cruzel, cruel, crudel*.

solh or *suelh* < *sŏleo*. This modal verb (< *sŏlēre*) is continued in Spanish and Italian, but has dropped from French where habitual acts are expressed through various syntactic and lexical devices, such as the use of the imperfect tense or of periphrastic expressions like 'avoir l'habitude de', 'être accoutumé à'.

chaptener 'to protect, to support' is derived from a combination of *capu* and *tenēre*. As a reflexive verb, it means 'to behave': *en qual manieyra se deu hom captener* (Appel: Chr., 115, 272). Derived from this verb are several nouns: *captenh* and the suffixated forms *captenensa* and *captenemen*, all with the meaning of 'behavior'.

Pois vei c'una pro no m'en te vas leis que.m destrui e.m cofon, totas las dopt' e las mescre, car be sai c'atretals se son. 'Since I see that nobody supports me against the lady who kills and destroys me, I fear them all and am suspicious of them, for I know very well that they are all the same.'

te or *ten* < *tĕnet*.

destrui < *destrūgit* is regularly developed; cf. *fūgit* > *fui*; *tragit* (for CL *trahit*) > *trai*. Analogical from these cases are verbs like *fai, plai*.

---

[78] Cf. Appel, § 56a; and Rohlfs, p. 77.

cofon < *confŭndit*. *N* was lost in Vulgar Latin, not only before *s* (CL *mensa* > VL *mesa*), but also before *v* and *f*: *ĭnfante* > *efan*, *enfan*; *convĕnīre* > *covenir, convenir*; *cofondre, cofessar, ifern*, etc. In French, the prefixes *con-* and *en-*, thus affected, have mostly been restored.[79]

dopt' < *dŭbĭto*. The supporting vowel is here elided before a word beginning with a vowel. Normally, final *o* is lost: *dīco* > *dic*, but certain consonant clusters require a supporting vowel: *cobre, tremble, dopte*. Quite frequently, this vowel is *-i* and not *-e*: *cobri, obri, suefri*; Anglade even considers *-i* the more common of the two endings. Also characteristic of Provençal is the early expansion of supporting vowels to positions where no such vowel seems required: *azori* (< *adōro*), *sospire, trobi*.[80] The primary cluster *bt* is reduced to *t*: *sŭbtīle* > *sotil*; *sŭbtus* > *sotz*. The development of the secondary *b't* group is far more complex and hesitant. Depending on whether the syncopation is an early or late occurrence, we get *pt* or *bd* (with intervocalic voicing preceding the loss of the weak vowel): *dŭbĭtare* > *doptar* (cf. Fr. *douter* and Sp. *dudar*); *cŭbĭtu* > *cobde* (cf. Old French which has both *coude* and *coute*); *sabbatu* > *sabde* and *sapte*. In addition to the problem concerning the date of the syncopation, we find cases of vocalization of the labial to *u̯*: *dēbĭtu* > *deute* and *deude*; *male habĭtu* > *malaut*. For this

---

[79] Grafström (§ 79) suggests that the graphical hesitation between *efant* and *effant* could represent a fluctuation in pronunciation; we would have: *ĭnfante* > *effant* > *efant*, with an assimilation of *nf* to *ff*, which is then simplified to *f*. He admits, however, that this assimilation could go back to Latin; *f* and *ff* are thus most likely mere graphical variants in Provençal.

[80] Cf. Anglade, p. 269; Schultz-Gora, § 130; and Appel, § 42b. Grandgent (§ 164) derives *-i* from verbs like *ai, vei, dei*, a theory which is later adopted by Ronjat. Grafström (§ 9, 7 and Morph., §§ 53-55) presents a very detailed discussion of this entire problem. He concludes that a change of *-e* to *-i* in hiatus with a subsequent spread to a more general use seems to offer the most plausible explanation of the phenomenon. The extended use of a final vowel *-e* or *-i* in the 1. pers. sing. of *-are* verbs outside of the type *tremble*, is seen as caused not only by an analogy with *tremble*, but rather by the need for a more harmonious paradigm. The 1. pers. sing. of the pres. ind. of *-are* verbs is isolated in the paradigm through its lack of any characteristic ending (*canto* > *cant*), and further phonological changes of the final consonant or consonantal cluster often removes the 1. pers. sing. even more from the general equilibrium of the paradigm (cf. *canto* > *cant* > *can*; *dōno* > *don* > *do*; *laudo* > *lau*; versus *cantas* > *cantas*; *dōnas* > *donas*; *laudas* > *lauzas*).

last word, varying forms such as *malapte, malaute* and *malaude* have all been attested.

atretals < *alteru tales*, which should have given * *altretals*. The loss of the first *l* comes about through dissimilation (cf. *flēbĭle* > *feble* and Fr. *faible*), and this feature then spreads to other combinations with *alteru*: *atretan, atressi*.

D'aisso.s fa be femna parer ma domna, per qu'e.lh o retrai, car no vol so c'om deu voler, e so c'om li deveda, fai. 'In this respect, my lady behaves like all women, and that is why I blame her for it, for she does not want what one should, and she does what is forbidden.'

fa is analogical from *esta* < *stat* and *da* < *dat*. The standard form is *fai* which appears in v. 36, and which, in turn, may change *esta* and *da* to *estai* and *dai*.

parer < *parēre*. Old French has *paroir*. The inchoative form of the infinitive, *parescĕre*, gives *pareiser* and Fr. *paraître*. The 3. pers. sing. of the pres. ind. of this verb is *par* and *pareis*, from *paret* and *parescit* respectively. Compare Old Fr. *pert* and Fr. *paraît*.

.lh is the enclitic dative form of *li* < *ĭllī*; *o* is from *hŏc*.

retrai is from *retraire*, a compound verb of VL * *tragĕre* for CL *trahĕre*. The 1. pers. sing. of the pres. ind., * *trago*, is mostly continued as *trai*, but the pohonological outcome is *trac* (cf. *Hugo* > *Uc*) which is recommended by the *Leys d'Amors*. *Trai* is drawn from an analogy with numerous 1. pers. sing. forms ending in *-i*: *ai, vei, crei, cai*, etc., some of which are themselves analogical. Another variant is *trau*, based on *dau* < * *da-o* < *do* and *estau* < * *sta-o* < *sto*.

deu < *dēbet*. A *b* which becomes final is vocalized to u; this is also the case with *-v*: *nave* > *nau*.

Chazutz sui en mala merce, et ai be faih co.l fols en pon; e no sai per que m'esdeve, mas car trop puyei contra mon. 'I have been dismissed from favor, and I have, indeed, acted like the mad man on the bridge, and I do not know why this is happening to me, if it is not because I wanted to ascend too high.'

chazuts is the past participle of *chazer, cazer* < VL *cadēre* < CL *cadĕre*. Vulgar Latin creates a large number of past participles in *-ūtu* which becomes the characteristic ending of *e* conjugation participles (cf. It. *veduto, caduto, bevuto*). Very few Classical Latin participles end in *-ūtu* (*solūtum, trĭbūtum*); its astounding expansion in Vulgar Latin is largely prompted by the perfect formation in *-ui*, although *-ūtu* is by no means limited to that category. In this example, *ūtu* is added to the stem of the infinitive and the present: *caz-er, caz-em*, but the close formal relationship between the perfect and the past participle accounts for the numerous instances of *-ūtu* added to the perfect stem. For *cazer*, we find *cazegutz* with a root based on *cazec*, alternate form of *cazet*; other examples are: *tolgut, tengut, vengut, valgut, pogut*, etc. [81]

sui. CL *sŭm* is replaced, in Vulgar Latin, by * *sŭjo*, modeled on * *aio* < *habeo*. Provençal has *soi* and *sui*, the change to *u* in *sui* being caused by the following yod (cf. similarly obtained *ūstiu* from *ōstiu*). Nyrop's assumption (encountered also in Schultz-Gora, Anglade and Grandgent) of an analogical influence from the perfect *fui* is now mostly abandoned, though still accepted by Lausberg. Meyer-Lübke and Fouché propose a change from *sŭm* to * *sŏyo*, but admit that the open *o* is unexplained. Provençal also has the regular outcome of *sŭm*: *son, so*, with an unstable *n*. [82]

faih < *factu*. *H* and *ih* are mere graphs for the sound [*tš*], usually represented by *-g* or *-ch*: *fag, fach*.

co.l fols en pon. This is an old saying, according to which a wise man descends from his horse when crossing a bridge. *Pon* is from *pŏnte*.

esdeve is the 3. pers. sing. of the pres. ind. of *esdevenir*.

---

[81] For the expansion of the *-ūtu* participle in Romance, see Lausberg, §§ 911-912; Väänänen, § 341; and Rohlfs: Hist. Gr., § 622.

[82] Cf. Lausberg, § 882; Rohlfs, p. 136 and note 351; Crescini, p. 113; and Fouché: Verbe, § 220.

puyei is the 1. pers. sing. of the perf. ind. of *puyar* < *pŏdiāre*, a derivation of *pŏdiu*. In pretonic position, *o* is often closed to *u*; the graph *y* may represent a yod or [dž]. Appel's chrestomathy gives the form *pogei* here.

Merces es perduda, per ver, (et eu non o saubi anc mai), car cilh qui plus ne degr' aver, no.n a ges, et on la querrai? 'Compassion is truly lost, (and I never knew it), for she who ought to feel compassion more than anybody else, does not harbor any, and where shall I go search for it?'

merces. Abstract nouns carry no article in Provençal, nor in Old French. The article appears, of course, if the noun is further determined by a prepositional construction or a relative clause: *la merces qu'ieu l'ai clamada* (Appel: Chr., 14,30). *Merces* does not continue CL *mĕrces*, but is either drawn from a VL * *mercēdis* or based on the accusative *mercé* (< *mercēde*) to which a flexional *s* is added.

saubi is a weak perfect form of *sapui*, alternating with the regular strong form *saup*; cf. *agui*, weak equivalent of *ac* < *habui*.

cilh. Surprising, in Provençal, is the use of *cilh, cist, ilh* as feminines along with the regular continuations of *ecce-ĭlla* > *cela*; *ecce-ĭsta* > *cesta*; *ĭlla* > *ela*. They are analogical from the relative pronoun *qui* which, in Vulgar Latin, came to be used in both genders, completely replacing the fem. *quae*.

degr' is an elided form of *degra* < *debuerat*. The pluperfect ind. of Classical Latin is continued in Provençal with the value of a conditional; it has also survived in Spanish, Portuguese and Old Italian in various modal-temporal usages, but has left few traces in Old French where it is limited to some of the oldest texts (Old Fr. *auret, pouret,* etc. < *habuerat, potuerat*). This conditional is built on the root of the perfect; compare also the role of the perfect in changing the corresponding first conjugation conditional *canta(v)eram* > *cantara* to *cantęra*, which has the open *e* of *perdęi, cantęi*. Grandgent terms this an "old" conditional, yet, surprisingly enough, there are no instances of it in the deeds. It is replaced, in the 13th - 14th century, by the "normal" conditional (the infinitive combined with the imperfect of *habēre*), except for the common forms *agra* and *fora* (< *habueram, fŭeram*) which survived much longer.[83]

.n is the enclitic form of *en* < *ĭnde*.

ges < *gĕnus* is commonly used as a negation; a variant, *gis*, owes its *i* to proclitic usage.

querrai < **quaerĕre aio*. With the exception of *ĕro*, the Classical Latin synthetic future did not survive in Romance; it was replaced by a new analytical future, consisting of the infinitive followed by the present tense of *habēre* (other auxiliaries are used in certain areas of Romania): **cantare aio* > *cantarai*; **cantare as* > *cantaras*, etc. The endings are thus identical with the present tense of the auxiliary, except that the *av-* portion is dropped in *avem, avetz* to give *cantarem, cantaretz*. Characteristic of Provençal is the syncopation of *i* in the future formation of *-ire* verbs: **partire aio* > *partrai* and also an analogical *partirai*, influenced by the infinitive *partir* just like in French. The *e* verbs syncopate: **quaerĕre aio* > *querrai*; **volēre aio* > *volrai*, while, in the *-are* group, *a* is quite regularly kept: *cantarai*. Sporadic occurrences of the insertion, between infinitive and ending, of weak pronouns and adverbs, indicate that the two constituent elements of the future formation could still be treated as separable units in Provençal: *e dir-vos-ai per que* 'and I shall tell you why' (Appel: Chr., 36,16); *dar-vos-em fromen* 'we shall give you some wheat' (ib., 51,36); *e trobar-n'i-a .xiii.* 'and he will find thirteen of them there' (ib., 115,317). This syntax is also found in Old Spanish, and it has kept its full vitality in Portuguese: *comprá-lo hei* 'I will buy it'.[84]

A! can mal sembla, qui la ve, qued aquest chaitiu deziron que ja ses leis non aura be, laisse morir, que no l'aon! 'Alas, to whomever sees her, how impossible it seems that she would let this unhappy

---

[83] For the morphology of this second conditional and for its temporal-modal usage, see Lausberg, § 828. See also Grandgent, § 185; and Crescini, p. 122. For the few survivals of this tense in the oldest French texts, see Nyrop, vol. 2, § 34.

[84] For the future formation in Romance, see Lausberg, §§ 837-846.

man, devoured by passion, and who will find no joy without her, die without bringing him any help.'

chaitiu is based on a combination of *captīvu* and a Celtic root * *cacht* (cf. Engl. *caught*), giving * *cactīvu* with a *ct* cluster; compare Fr. *chétif*.

ses < *sĭne* + *s*. Many Latin adverbs end in *-s*: *mĕlius*, *pĕius*, *prius*, etc., with the result that *-s* came to be considered a normal adverbial ending and was added to numerous adverbs and prepositions in Provençal as well as in Old French. In Provençal, it even spreads to the adverbial formation in *-men*, where we find an etymological *longamen* (< *lŏngā mĕnte*) alternating with *longamens* and *longamentz*.

aon < *abŭndet* is the 3. pers. sing. of the pres. subj.; the subjunctive mood is here governed by *que no*. *B* is lost before a back vowel.

Pus ab midons no.m pot valer precs ni merces ni.l dreihz qu'eu ai, ni a leis no ven a plazer qu'eu l'am, ja mais no.lh o dirai. 'Since, with my lady, prayers nor mercy nor the rights I have cannot help me, and since it does not please her that I love her, I shall never tell her again.'

midons and *sidons* (* *tidons* does not exist) are fossilized vocatives, morphologically masculine, but functioning as feminines in the troubadour poetry, since the lady was considered a feudal lord, whom the lover-poet served and obeyed. These forms are invariable regardless of their syntactic function. [85]

pot < *pŏtet* is a singular; this lack of agreement is almost the rule when the subject is composed of coordinated nouns which follow the verb. There is agreement with the first noun only; cf. *e crec sos sens e sos sabers e sos trobars e sa gaillardia e sa drudaria* (Boutière, p. 76, 11-12).

precs is drawn from *pregar*; it is a post-verbal noun.

---

[85] Crescini (pps. 86-87) mentions the possibility of *mi* being a proclitic reduction of *meus* (cf. Fr. *monsieur* with a weakened *mon*).

dreihz < *directus*. The *ct* cluster gives [tš] in some regions, in others it. The [tš] sound, as has already been observed, is spelled in a variety of ways: *factu* > *fag, fach, fah, faih, faich*. When a flexional *s* (frequently *z* after a palatal) is added, the resulting sound combination is rather complex and difficult to pronounce and is consequently reduced to [tš] or [ts]. Grafström indicates that [tš] itself may develop into [ts], and he cannot decide whether *fach* was pronounced with "[ts] ou un phonème s'acheminant de [ty] ou [tš] vers [ts]." Followed by a flexional *s*, there was a strong tendency for [tšs] to simplify to [ts], as seen from rhymes like *malfagz - alumenatz*; the complex spelling *fagz* instead of *faz* could be linked with the singular *fag*. [86]

Aissi.m part de leis e.m recre; mort m'a, e per mort li respon, e vau m'en, puis ilh no.m rete, chaitius, en issilh, no sai on. 'Thus I leave her in despair; she has killed me, and I answer her like a dead man, and since she does not retain me, I shall go into exile, an unhappy man, I do not know where.'

recre. The verb *recreire* (< *recrēdĕre*) denotes fatigue or refusal, renouncement; Meyer-Lübke translates it 'den Mut verlieren, sich für besiegt erklären.' This meaning of fatigue, of abandoning something disheartedly, is clearly shown in the following line: *car m'era de chan recrezutz* 'for I had grown weary of singing.' [87]

vau comes from *vado*, changed to **vao* under the influence of *do* > **da-o* > *dau* and *sto* > **sta-o* > *estau*, forms which show restoration of the stem-vowel *a* (*da-s* and *da-t* give an analogical *da-o*) and the subsequent change of the *o* ending into the second element of the *au* diphthong. Compare CL *ĕgo* > VL *ĕo* > *eu, ieu*.

ilh appears here as a feminine pronoun; parallel cases are the demonstratives *cist* and *cilh*.

issilh < *exĭliu*. Provençal has *eissilh* and *eisselh* alongside with *issilh*; this latter form shows a pretonic weakening, common in the

---

[86] See a detailed interpretation of these various graphs in Grafström, § 71, 2-3.
[87] Cf. REW 2307 *crēdĕre*.

language, of *ei-* to *i-* (cf. *examen* > *eissam, issam*). With a Latin etymon in *-ĭliu, -elh* represents the phonological outcome. Appel derives *-ilh* from an analogy with the verb *exīre* > *eissir, issir*; it could, of course, also be a regional form, characteristic of areas where a palatal can raise *e* to *i*.[88]

Tristans, ges no.n auretz de me, qu'eu m'en vau, chaitius, no sai on. De chantar me gic e.m. recre, e de joi e d'amor m'escon. 'Tristan, you shall hear no more of me, for I am leaving, an unhappy man, for an unknown destination. I am giving up singing, and I seek refuge against joy and love.'

Tristans is an example of a *senhal*, a name that was coined primarily (though perhaps not in this particular instance) with a view to concealing the lady's identity. The troubadour, courting a married lady of high social rank, was confronted with enemies: the *gilós* (the husband, who is referred to as "jealous") and the *lausengiers* (the husband's entourage or "flatterers"); consequently, he was forced to use caution and even the art of dissimulation in his poems. Following are a few characteristic examples of *senhals*, referring to a lady whose identity is thus covered up: *Bel Vezer, Sobrepretz, Rosa Gentil, Mon Cortes, Bel Cavalier*; they usually appear in the refrain (*tornada*). In other instances, a *senhal* was used for the lord whom the troubadour served, and it could also refer to the *joglar* in case the troubadour wanted to give him valuable advice concerning the declamation of the poem. This versatility often makes it well-nigh impossible to penetrate the mystery of the *senhals*. A further complication is the conventional

---

[88] For the weakening of pretonic *ei-* to *-i*, see Rohlfs, pps. 162-163, note 431. A detailed description of the simplification of diphthongs is offered by Grafström (§§ 5-7), and supplemented by M. Pfister, in *Vox Romanica*, vol. 17, 1958, pps. 290-303. Appel (§ 37) ascribes the change of *ei-* to *i-* to the influence of *s*. The impact of stem-stressed forms (ex. Old Fr. *ist* < *ĕxit*) on pretonic *ei-* is mentioned by Rheinfelder (§ 249); this explanation is, however, of a somewhat restricted validity, since it applies to verbs only. For the influence of *exīre* on *exĭliu*, see Appel, §§ 33d and 66d. The raising influence of a palatal is offered as an explanation by Crescini (pps. 7-8). Finally, it should be mentioned that the continuation of *ĭ* as *i* is a characteristic feature of learned words: *famĭlia* > *familha*, Fr. *famille*; compare also Fr. *exil*.

use of the masculine gender referring to the lady in her role as the poet's feudal lord; cf. *Bel Cavalier* and compare the use of *midons* in the courtly love poetry. In the case of *Tristans*, it is not quite clear whether this *senhal* refers to a lady or to a friend or *joglar*, or whether it is an allusion to the Tristan legend. Some scholars consider it a reference to the troubadour Raimbaut d'Aurenga.[89]

gic comes from *gequir* < *jehjan; the variant *giquir* shows influence of the initial palatal. The change of Germanic *h* to *k* is unaccounted for.[90]

---

[89] For the role of the *senhal* in troubadour poetry, see S. Strónski: *le Troubadour Folquet de Marseille*, Krakow, 1910, pps. 27-43; Jeanroy, vol. 1, pps. 317-320; and Riquer, pps. XXXII-XXXIII. A list of *senhals* is given by F. Bergert: "Die von den Trobadors genannten oder gefeierten Damen," in *ZRPh*, Beihef 46, Halle, 1913.

[90] Cf. REW 4580 *jehjan*, where Meyer-Lübke states: "Die lautlichen Verhältnisse sind nicht klar." Appel (§ 46a) compares the loss of Germanic *h* in * *spehon* > *espiar* with its change to *k* in *gequir*.

2. LA COMTESSA DE DIA: *A chantar m'er de so
    q'ieu no volria.*

I.   A chantar m'er de so q'ieu no volria,
      tan me rancur de lui cui sui amia
      car eu l'am mais que nuilla ren que sia;
      vas lui no.m val merces ni cortesia,
5   ni ma beltatz, ni mos pretz, ni mos sens,
      c'atressi.m sui enganad', e trahia
      cum degr' esser, s'ieu fos desavinens.

II.   D'aisso.m conort car anc non fi faillenssa,
      amics vas vos per nuilla captenenssa,
10   anz vos am mais non fetz Seguis Valenssa,
      e platz mi mout qez eu d'amor vos venssa,
      lo mieus amics, car etz lo plus valens;
      mi faitz orguoill en digz et en parvenssa
      et si etz francs vas totas autras gens.

15 III.   Meravill me cum vostre cors s'orguoilla,
      amics, vas me, per q'ai razon qe.m duoilla;
      non es ges dreitz c'autr' amors vos mi tuoilla
      per nuilla ren qe.us diga ni.us acuoilla;
      e membre vos cals fo.l comensamens
20   de nostr' amor, ja Dompnidieus non vuoilla
      q.en ma colpa sia.l departimens!

IV.   Proesa grans q'el vostre cors s'aizina
      e lo rics pretz q'avetz m'en atayna,
      c'una non sai loindana ni vezina

25   si vol amar vas vos non si'aclina;
          mas vos, amics, etz ben tant conoisens
          que ben devetz conoisser la plus fina,
          e membre vos de nostres covinens.

    V. Valer mi deu mos pretz e mos paratges
30   e ma beutatz e plus mos fis coratges,
          per q'ieu vos mand lai on es vostr' estatges
          esta chansson que me sia messatges:
          e voill saber, lo mieus bels amics gens,
          per que vos m'etz tant fers ni tant salvatges,
35   non sai si s'es orguoills o mals talens.

    VI. Mas aitan plus vuoill qe.us diga.l messatges
          q'en trop d'orguoill an gran dan maintas gens.

A chantar m'er de so qu'ieu no volria, tant me rancur de lui cui sui amia car eu l'am mais que nuilla ren que sia 'I shall have to sing about what I would rather not sing about, so much do I hold a grudge against him whose friend I am, for I love him more than anything in the world.'

m'er, from *mihi ĕrit*, is an impersonal construction denoting obligation. *Er* is a continuation of the Latin future *ĕrit*, also preserved in Old French. It is not attested in any plural form at all in Provençal, which seems to indicate that this last remaining Classical Latin future was on its way out already in preliterary times, hard pressed by the Romance formation * *(es)sĕre aio* > *serai*.

volria < *volēre (h)abe(b)am* is a conditional, formed from a combination of the infinitive with the imperfect of *habēre*. The insertion of a *d* in *l'r* and *n'r* clusters is not as general as in French, but rather it is optional in Provençal and is fairly rare with *l'r*: *tĕneru* > *tenre* and *tendre*; *tŏllĕre* > *tolre* and *toldre*; *honorare* > *onrar* and *ondrar*.

rancur. The noun *rancōre* is continued as Pr. *rancor*, It. *rancore* and Sp. *rencor*. Other continuations in Gallo-Romance as well as Hispano-Romance point to an early influence of *cūra*: Pr. Pg. *rancura*, Sp. *rencura*, Old Fr. *rancure* and Fr. *rancune*. The verb is *rancurar*; it appears here in the 1. pers. sing. of the pres. ind. [91]

cui functions as a genitive here, being the equivalent of Fr. *dont*.

---

[91] Cf. REW 7041 *rancor*. Meyer-Lübke obtains Fr. *rancune* through a dissimilation with initial *r*; to this should possibly be added some influence of *n*.

amia < *amīca*. Normally, intervocalic *c* before *a* is voiced to *g*: *amiga*; *prĕcāre > *pregar*; *mīca* > *miga*. The change of *c* to *i̯* represents a dialectal variant, characteristic of the Limousin region; the pronunciation may have been [j] rather than [dž], although an assibilation cannot be ruled out: *pacare* > *pagar* and *paiar*; *prĕcāre > *pregar* and *preiar*; *amīca* > *amiga* and *amiia > *amia*, with absorption of the yod by the vowel *i*. The form *miia* (< *mīca*) is attested in the earliest Provençal text, the *Boeci*; elsewhere, we find *miga* and *mia*. *Dīcam* (subjunctive of *dire*) > *diga* and *dia*. [92]

mais < *magis* is used here in a comparative function. Synthetic comparatives of Classical Latin (*aptior, fortior*, etc.) were to a large extent replaced, in the popular language, by analytical formations with *plus* or *magis* (*plus* or *magis aptus*). It should be noted that the construction with *magis* existed already in Classical Latin with a few adjectives ending in *-us*: *magis idoneus, magis arduus*. Gallo-, Italo- and Rheto-Romance adopted *plus*, whereas Roumanian and Hispano-Romance continued *magis*. While *plus* is normally used in Provençal to form the comparative of adjectives (*plus cortes, plus avinens*), *mais* appears quite frequently in other comparative functions: *ja mais, no mais, mais de dos cens* 'more than 200,' *amar mais*, etc. Compare also *no.n puesc mais* which has, as its exact counterpart, the somewhat archaic French idiom *je n'en puis mais* 'I cannot take it any longer.' *Magis* is found before an adjective in the Gascon stanza of Raimbaut de Vaqueiras' multilingual *descort*: *coar sotz la mes bon'e bera* (Hamlin, 53, 26). Notice also the comparative function of *mielhs* in the following example where *trop mielhs* is the equivalent of Fr. *bien plus*: *e'n˚Raymbautz, quant ab armas s'eslansa, sembla trop mielhs ioglars que cavalliers* (Appel: Chr., 98, 59-60).

ren < *rĕm*. Final *m* in monosyllables is kept as an unstable *n*: *sŭm* > *son, so*; *mĕum* > *mom > *mon, mo*. An exception is *iam* which is continued only as *ja*; cf. Sp. *ya*, Old Fr. *ja*.

vas lui no.m val merces ni cortesia, ni ma beltatz, ni mos pretz, ni mos sens, c'atressi.m sui enganad' e trahia cum degr' esser, s'ieu fos

---

[92] Crescini (p. 26) relates this feature to the treatment of initial *ca* - and *ga*-.

desavinens. 'With him, neither compassion nor courtesy nor my beauty nor my merit nor my intelligence are of any avail, for I have been deceived and betrayed, as much as I would have been, had I been a disagreeable person.'

vas < *vĕrsu* reflects the normal Vulgar Latin assimilation of *rs* to *s*, but is otherwise a proclitic word showing some fluctuation in the treatment of the vowel: *ves, vas* and also *vers*; cf. Old Sp. *viesso* and the learned modern form *verso*.

val < *valet*. As usual in enumerations, agreement is made with the closest noun only.

beltatz comes from * *bĕllĭtātis*, or else it is drawn from the accusative *beltat* < * *bēllĭtāte* through the addition of a flexional *s*. The imparisyllabic flexion: * *bĕllĭtas* - *bĕllĭtāte* is eliminated.

pretz < *prĕtiu*. When final, *tį* evolves to a voiceless [*ts*], spelled *tz*: *palatiu* > *palatz*. Intervocalically, it gives a voiced *s*: * *prĕtiare* > *prezar*.

enganaď < * *ĭngannāta* is listed by Appel as a word of unknown or uncertain origin. With *g* in syllable initial position, this word may show the usual fluctuation between [*g*] and [*dž*] before *a*, although *enjanar* is fairly rare. Somewhat more common is the noun *enjan* as an alternate of *engan*.

trahia < * *tradīta*. A regular development of this participle gives *trazida* and also *traïda*, since intervocalic *d* may drop. The loss of intervocalic *t* is unaccounted for; *h* serves the same function as a dieresis, that of separating two vowels in hiatus (compare Fr. *trahir* and *naïf*).

esser < VL *essĕre* < CL *esse*. Quite frequently, Provençal will drop the final vowel and keep the weak post-tonic non-final vowel instead: *carcĕre* > *carcer*; * *cassanu* > *casse(r)*. This is particularly common wiht infinitives in *-ĕre*: *co(g)noscĕre* > *conoisser*; *plangĕre* > *planher*; * *nascĕre* > *naisser*. It is probably this peculiar stress pattern that has kept Provençal from carrying the insertion of glides (transitional consonants) as far as did French.

desavinens. Avinen (Fr. *avenant*) is derived from the verb *advĕnīre*. The intertonic or *contrefinale* vowel is usually weakened or lost, and the weakening results in a hesitation between *e* and *i* in that position: *avinen* and *avenen*; *entendimen* and *entendemen*. Compare also the use of both *e* and *i* as supporting vowels: *cobre* and *cobri*. Retention of the weak vowel is often brought about through analogy with other forms of the word involved: *finír* and *finimén*; *oblít* and *oblidár*.

D'aisso.m conort car anc non fi faillenssa, amics vas vos per nuilla captenenssa, anz vos am mais non fetz Seguis Valenssa. 'I draw comfort from the thought that I never deserted you, my friend, in my conduct towards you, on the contrary, I love you more than Seguin did Valensa.'

conort. CL *cohŏrtāri* 'to exhort, encourage, esp. about troops' > VL *conhŏrtāre* > *conortar* 'to exhort, encourage, comfort, console.' Quite similar in both form and meaning is *confŏrtāre* 'to strengthen, comfort, console,' a derivation, in ecclesiastical Latin, of the adjective *fŏrtis*, and which is continued as It. *confortare* and Pr. Cat. Sp. Pg. *confortar*. A confusion between these two verbs proved inevitable in Romance, as shown by this very early example of Old Fr. *conforter* as the equivalent of Pr. *conortar* and Lat. *cohortari*: *cio confortent ad ambos duos que sent ralgent in lor honors* 'they exhort both of them to go back to their posts' (*la Vie de Saint Léger*, v. 20e-f). [93]

fi < *fēcī*. The *i* is obtained through *umlaut*, and *fēcī* should thus give *fitz*; *fis*, which is the normal form, is analogical from *mis, pris, quis*. *Fi* could possibly come from an analogy with *vi* < *vīdī*. [94]

---

[93] Cf. REW 2147 * *conhŏrtāre* and 2138 *confŏrtāre*.
[94] Cf. Crescini, p. 117. Grafström (Morph., § 66) finds the analogy with *vi* an insufficient reason for the creation of *fi*; instead, he links it with the reduction of *fetz* to *fe* under the influence of *de* < *dĕdit*, a simple vocalic difference being the only feature that separates the two longer forms.

anz < VL **antius* < CL *antea*. The Vulgar Latin form is analogical from *prius*. Old French usually has *ainz* with an unexplained release of yod. The word marks a strong contrast, corresponds to German *sondern*, with *mais* being the equivalent of the weaker *aber*.

fetz < *fēcit* is the 3. pers. sing. of the perf. ind. It functions here as *verbum vicarium*, taking up the verb *am* of the main clause. *Fetz* is not introduced by any conjunction; we have a case of parataxis, a common construction in the medieval period which consists of the placing of clauses one after the other, without any formal words to indicate coordination or subordination. In the following example: *eu non posc mudar, no chan* (Appel: Chr., 18b, 4), the subjunctive *chan* (< *cantem*) is governed by *non posc mudar* in spite of the lack of a conjunction. Subordination is also evident from the use of the subjunctive *siatz* in this example: *aurs ni argens no.us garra, non siatz pendutz* (ib., 3, 436-437).

Seguis-Valenssa. *Seguis* is the subject of *fetz*, *Valenssa* the object. This is a reference to characters in a novel that has long been lost; they are also mentioned in a poem by Arnaut de Maruelh.

e platz mi mout qez eu d'amor vos venssa, lo mieus amics, car etz lo plus valens; mi faitz orguoill en digz et en parvenssa et si etz francs vas totas autras gens. 'and I am very happy to be superior to you in love, my friend, for you are worthier than I; towards me, you are haughty in words and in behavior, yet you are friendly towards everybody else.'

qez < *quĭd* or *quod* used before a vowel so as to give an intervocalic *d*. The same case of syntactic phonetics obtains with *ad* > *az* and, by analogy, with *et* > *ez*.

The retention of a minimal opposition through a linguistic economy measure seems unduly complicated and is itself viewed as insufficient, for Grafström quickly adds that "*vi* (< *vīdī*) a pu soutenir *fi*". Nor does he seem to have given proper consideration to the fact that the true opposition was that of *fis* versus *fetz*.

venssa is derived from *venser* < *vĭncĕre*, of which it keeps the root *vens-*; however, an etymological subjunctive *venca* (< *vĭncam*) is also encountered, and this root is kept in the past participle *vencut* and in the perfect *venquei*.

etz < *ĕstis*. The cluster *st's* is normally reduced to *tz*; we have a similar reduction of *sc's* to *cs*: *quĭsquĭs* > *quecs*.

orguoill < Germanic * *ŭrgōli*. The diphthongization here as well as in Fr. *orgueil* points to the Germanic *ō* as having been equated with an open vowel, since a close *o* cannot undergo such changes. [95]

parvenssa. In Italian, there are instances of *u̯* going to *v* when a liquid *r* or *l* precedes: *parui* > It. *parvi*; *dŏluit* > Old It. *dolve*; and this can then be followed up by a subsequent analogical penetration of *v* into other forms and derivations of the verb *parere*: It. *parvente* (and also *parvenza*) versus CL *parente*. In Provençal, where *-ui* perfects turn into the characteristic *c* and *g* forms (*ac, aguist*), and where *parer* is attested only with a weak perfect, *parec* (with an analogical *-ec* for *-et*), a similar explanation of *parven* does not seem possible. A direct analogy from *ferven* and *serven* is certainly more plausible than an isolated occurrence of *u̯* > *v* in a hypothetic * *paru̯ente* for CL *parente*.

francs < Frankish * *frank* (+ *-s*), a proper name with wich the Franks designated themselves, and which was early Latinized to *Francus*. As an adjective, it was mostly used with the meaning 'free' in the Middle Ages, but it soon came to denote a variety of

---

[95] Cf. REW 9084 *ŭrgōli*. Manuel Alvar, in his book on the Aragonese dialect, lists * *ŭrgōli* > Aragonese *orgüello* among a handful of examples that lead him to suspect that even close vowels could diphthongize in that dialect: "Se podría sospechar ... que en aragonés las vocales cerradas han podido, también, diptongar" (M. Alvar López: *El dialecto aragonés*, Madrid: Gredos, 1953, § 79, 2). A comparison with the Gallo-Romance forms should have convinced him that this particular example is far from irreproachable. Corominas makes specific mention of the open quality of Germanic long *o*: "la *o* larga germánica tenía timbre abierto, y como tal se reproduce en romance"; see Corominas, art. *orgullo*. Sp. *orgullo* is a borrowing from Cat. *orgull*; Catalan regularly closes *ŏ* to *u* before a palatal: *ŏculu* > *ull*.

good qualities such as 'frank, sincere, good, friendly, pure, noble'. Introduced into French, it quickly spread to other Romance languages: Pr. *franc*, It. Sp. Pg. *franco*.

Meravill me cum vostre cors s'orguoilla, amics, vas me, per q'ai razon qe.m duoilla; non es ges dreitz c'autr' amors vos mi tuoilla per nuilla ren qe.us diga ni.us acuoilla 'My friend, I wonder why you should be arrogant towards me; it is with good reason that I am sad; it is unjust that another love should take you away from me for anything that I may say or grant you.'

vostre cors. It is often hard to determine whether *cors* comes from *cor* + a flexional *s*, or whether it goes back to *cŏrpus*. The use of *cors* for emphasis ('my body' = 'I') is widespread in Gallo-Romance.

duoilla and *tuoilla* are subjunctives regularly derived from *dŏleat* and * *tŏlleat*, with an optional diphthongization and with *ill* as a graph for palatal *l*.

vos mi. Hamlin quotes this example as proof of a different word order from that of modern French, but a combination of *vous* and *me* is altogether impossible in French yet not uncommon in Provençal. [96]

nuilla is only negative when accompanied by a negation. In this passage, it has the indefinite meaning of 'whatever, anything'; cf. *ieu chan mielhs de nulh autre chantador* (Appel: Chr., 16, 1-2.)

acuoilla is the 1. pers. sing. of the pres. subj. of *acolhir* < * *ad-colligĕre*, which has undergone an early change in conjugation; cf. Fr. *accueillir*. The palatal *l* stems from a combination of *l* and a prepalatal *g*: *cŏllĭgit* > *colh, cuolh, cuelh*, and is then generalized in the paradigm as the final root consonant. Phonologically, a palatal *l* could not develop in the subjunctive before an *a*, nor in the 1. pers. sing. of the pres. ind. before an *o*; compare It. *cogliere*,

---

[96] Cf. Hamlin, p. 142.

coglie versus *colga, colgo*. The combination of *l* and prepalatal *g* does not uniformly give a palatal *l*; one important exception is CL *fŭlgŭre* > VL * *fŭlgĕre* > *folzer, fouzer*, where a strong syllabic division seems to have prevented a merger of *l* and *g*. In this particular word, *l* is treated as final of syllable before a consonant, and *g*, initial of syllable following a liquid, becomes [dz] rather than [dž]. The notion of *cŏllĭgĕre* as being a compound of *legĕre* was lost at a relatively early stage, and no efforts were made towards a recomposition in Vulgar Latin. Compare CL *dísplĭcet* > VL * *displácet* > *desplatz, desplai* and Fr. *déplaît*.

e membre vos cals fo.l comensamens de nostr' amor, ja Dompnidieus non vuoilla q.en ma colpa sia.l departimens! 'and remember how our love began, and the Lord forbid that I have any guilt in our separation!'

e membre vos. The subjunctive makes it possible to express an order in an impersonal construction; the locution we have here is the equivalent of Fr. *qu'il vous souvienne*. The ind. is *membra* < *mĕmorat*; the subj. *membre* < *mĕmoret* shows the regular loss of *-et* and the addition of a supporting vowel.

ja introduces an independent optative subjunctive.

Dompnidieus < *dŏmine dĕus* shows retention of the weak vowel *e* as *i*. Provençal also has *dombredieus* with a treatment of the secondary *m'n* cluster that parallels that of Spanish; cf. *hŏmĭne* > Sp. *hombre*. *Domine* is a rare example of a vocative that has been kept in Gallo-Romance; compare the opening line of *la Vie de Saint Léger*: *Domine deu devemps lauder* as well as more popular continuations in Old French: *damedeu, damerdeu, dameldeu*, etc.

vuoilla < *vŏleat* is the pres. subj.; the pres. ind. is *vol* < *vŏlet*, and in the 1. pers. sing., our poem has both the diphthongized and the non-diphthongized form, *vuoill* and *voill* < *vŏleo*.

Proesa grans q'el vostre cors s'aizina e lo rics pretz q'avetz m'en atayna, c'una non sai loindana ni vezina si vol amar vas vos non si'aclina; *mas vos, amics, etz ben tant conoisens que ben devetz conoisser la plus fina, e membre vos de nostres covinens*. 'I am disturbed about the great prowess that you harbor in your chest, and about your great merit, for I do not know of any woman, distant or near, who would not yield to you, if she wants to fall in love. But you, my friend, are discerning enough to realize who is the most faithful; and do remember our vows!'

el is the enclitic continuation of *en lo*.

aizina. The verb *aizinar* 'arrange, accommodate, dwell' and the noun *aizina* 'utensil, vase, commodity' are derived from *adjacens*. According to Rohlfs, Pr. *aise* is a borrowing from French, but he admits that the French development itself is rather obscure; he suggest the following stages for this evolution: CL *adjacens* > VL * *ajaçe* > * *ájedze* > Fr. *aise*. Pfister likewise considers *aise* a French borrowing as opposed to a more indigenous *aitz*. Semantically, the word undergoes a series of changes from a purely local meaning, 'close by', to 'at hand', and then via 'ease' and 'comfort' to 'commodity' and 'utensil'. [97]

rics < Frankish * *rîki* (+ -*s*), a word which meant 'powerful', and which was often used with its original meaning in Provençal; cf. *nuls om vidist un rey tan ric* (Appel: Chr., 2, 12).

atayna is derived from Gothic * *tahjan*, possibly via an intermediate form * *taheins*, as suggested by Meyer-Lübke. [98]

loindana < *longĭtāna* owes its *d* to a late syncopation, allowing a voicing of intervocalic *t*; compare Fr. *lointain*. The graph *in* reflects a palatalized *n*.

---

[97] Cf. FEW, art. *adjacens*; REW 168 *adjacens*; Rohlfs, p 209; and M. Pfister, in *Vox Romanica*, vol. 18, 1959, pps. 240-246, who offers a very thorough description of *adjacens* and all its Provençal derivations. The difference Pfister establishes between *aissina* with a voiceless *s* ('demeure, dépendance'), derived from *aitz*, and *aizina* with a voiced *s* ('ustensile, occasion favorable'), based on *aise*, seems altogether too rigid, if one may judge from the verb *aizinar* 'arranger, accommoder', semantically very close to 'demeurer, loger': 'qui s'accommode en vous' > 'qui demeure en vous'.

[98] Cf. REW 8529a *tahjan*. Appel (§ 18) lists *ataïnar* as a word of unknown or uncertain origin.

nostres < *nostros*. Provençal has kept a full form, with *e* as a supporting vowel, as opposed to the strongly reduced Old Fr. acc. plur. *noz* (> Fr. *nos*).

Valer mi deu mos pretz e mos paratges e ma beutatz e plus mos fis coratges, per q'ieu vos mand lai on es vostr' estatges esta chansson que me sia messatges: 'My merit and my noble birth and my beauty and my faithful heart must render me some service; therefore, I send you, to your domicile, this poem as my messenger.'

paratges < * *paratĭcus*. The *-aticu* suffix gives *-atge* (also spelled *-atje*). Grandgent explains that *c* voices to *g*, then becomes [j̯] and moves on to [dž] when appearing between the last two vowels of a proparoxytone. The voiced result implies a late syncopation. *T* is kept, at least in spelling, but a complex group of [tdž] seems somewhat difficult to accept in pronunciation. Notice, in this respect, the developments suggested by Crescini of *viatĭcu*: > * *viadije* > * *viadje*, with *viatge* being a mere graph for this last form.[99]

fis and fem. *fina*, Fr. *fin*, It. *fino*, etc., do not have a Latin adjective as their etymon, but are drawn from the noun *finis* 'end', used very early in Latin in a figurative sense: 'the utmost, the most

---

[99] References to this thorny problem are numerous. Cf. Grandgent, § 65, G, 3; and Crescini, p. 54. Meyer-Lübke (*Das Katalanische*, Heidelberg, 1925, § 44) considers the non-palatalized *-atgue* to be indigenous and treats *-atge* as a French borrowing. Grafström (§ 70,1) arrives at *-atgue* via the chain: *-aticu* > * *-adego* > * *-adgo* > *-adgue* > *-atgue*. He concludes that *-atgue* may very well palatalize in Provençal to *-atge* and sees no need to explain the palatalized form as a French borrowing. He finds support for this theory in a brief statement by Menéndez Pidal (§ 84, I) to the effect that Sp. *-aje* (*salvaje, ramaje*) is of either Provençal or French origin. To this may be objected that Rohlfs (Hist. Gr., § 1060) derives It. *-aggio* (*coraggio, vantaggio*) exclusively from the French "Modesuffix" *-age*. It should further be pointed out that Menéndez Pidal, in the quoted passage, has devoted only a couple of lines to the history of the *-aticu* suffix in Spanish. For French, Rohlfs (p. 107) proposes the following chain of development: *-aticu* > * *-adegu* (late syncopation and voicing) > * *-adeu* (loss of *g* before *u* and creation of a secondary *di̯* cluster). The difficulty here is that *di̯* is normally reduced to *i̯*: *radiu* > *rai*; *pŏdiu* > *pui*, whereas the secondary *di̯* of * *-adeu* undergoes the same evolution as *bi̯*: *rŭbeu* > *rouge*. This is stressed by Lausberg (§ 524), who offers the same explanation for Provençal: "Im Provenzalischen verläuft die Entwicklung entsprechend."

perfect part of something': *finis honōrum* 'the highest of honors, the highest honor'. A transitional stage of this semantic change can still be observed in such French locutions as *le fin fond*. Engl. *fine* is borrowed from French.

mand < *mando*. Final *-nd* and *-nt* are normally reduced to a stable *n*: *mŭndu* > *mon*; *pŏnte* > *pon*. The form *mand* is easily justified as analogical from other forms of the same verb such as *mandar, manda, mandam*. Morphological pressure would thus quickly bring the unusual *man* < *mando* back into the fold, but it should be observed that our text has several examples of *tant* instead of *tan* < *tantu*, where no such morphological pressure exists: *tant conoisens, tant fers, tant salvatges*.[100]

e voill saber, lo mieus bels amics gens, per que vos m'etz tant fers ni tant salvatges, non sai si s'es orguoills o mals talens. 'and I would like to know, my dear friend, why you are so cruel and fierce to me, for I do not know whether it is haughtiness or lack of good faith.'

gens < *genĭtus*. This word originally meant 'born' (born into a family or clan, *gens*), then 'of noble birth' and finally 'nice, gracious, beautiful'. Similar changes have occurred in French for the word *gentil* which now means 'nice, pleasant', but which has kept its older meaning 'noble' in the compound *gentilhomme* 'nobleman'.

salvatges < *salvaticus* < *sĭlvaticus* represents a very early instance of a vocalic assimilation, attested in the *Glossary of Reichenau* which carries the following entry: *onager - asinus salvaticus*, and it appears even as early as the beginning of the 6th century, used by Anthimus to designate 'wild mulberries': *mora salvatica*.

mals is quite frequently found in adjectival function in Gallo-Romance: *ab sa mala doctrina*.

---

[100] Crescini (p. 56) asserts that *cuant* (< *quando, quantu*) is used before a vowel, *quan* elsewhere, yet it is clear that no such distribution has been observed for *tant* here. Grafström (§ 76, 3) mentions a rigorous distinction, in the dialect of Toulouse, between *cant* < *quantu* and *can* < *quàndo*.

Mas aitan plus vuoill qe.us diga.l messatges q'en trop d'orguoill an gran dan maintas gens. 'But even more so, I want my messenger to tell you that too much haughtiness makes many people suffer.'

aitan < *ac* + *tantu*. Similar combinations are found in other words of a demonstrative value: *aital, aicest, aicel. Ac* and *atque* were often used for emphasis in popular Latin.

an is the 3, pers. plur. of the pres. ind. of *aver*. The Classical Latin ending *-ent* (CL *habent*) was often replaced by *-unt* in Vulgar Latin: *habunt, debunt*, etc. VL *habunt*, with loss of *b* before a velar vowel, gives us *aun, au* and Fr. *ont. An* is analogical from *dan, estan* < *dant, stant*: or it may go back to a VL * *ant*.

maintas is also spelled *mantas* or *manhtas*, forms that show different graphical representations of palatalized *n*. The etymology of the word is not quite clear and has been much debated. Meyer-Lübke proposes a combination of *magnu* and *tantu*, which would account for the palatal *n* as well as for the final dental, and Rohlfs still believes this to be the most plausible explanation. Various Celtic or Germanic etymologies have been put forth; Thurneysen suggests a Gaulish * *mantî*, accepted by Grandgent, but rejected by Meyer-Lübke on phonological grounds. Gunnar Tilander derives *maint* from Old Frankish * *manichte*, a noun meaning 'crowd'. [101]

---

[101] Cf. REW 5231 *magnus*; and Rohlfs, p. 62.

3. GIRAUT DE BORNELH: *Reis glorios, verais lums e clartatz*

    I. Reis glorios, verais lums e clartatz,
        Deus poderos, Senher, si a vos platz,
        al meu companh siatz fizels aiuda;
        qu'eu no lo vi, pos la nochs fo venguda,
5   et ades sera l'alba!

    II. Bel companho, si dormetz o velhatz,
        no dormatz plus, suau vos ressidatz;
        qu'en orien vei l'estela creguda
        c'amena.l jorn, qu'eu l'ai be conoguda,
10   et ades sera l'alba!

    III. Bel companho, en chantan vos apel;
        no dormatz plus, qu'eu auch chantar l'auzel
        que vai queren lo jorn per lo boschatge
        et ai paor que.l gilos vos assatge,
15   et ades sera l'alba!

    IV. Bel companho, issetz al fenestrel
        e regardatz las estelas del cel!
        Conoisseretz si.us sui fizels messatge;
        si non o faitz, vostres n'er lo damnatge,
20   et ades sera l'alba!

    V. Bel companho, pos me parti de vos,
        eu no.m dormi ni.m moc de genolhos;
        ans preiei Deu, lo filh Santa Maria,
        que.us me rendes per leial companhia,
25   et ades sera l'alba!

VI. Bel companho, la foras als peiros
me preiavatz qu'eu no fos dormilhos,
enans velhes tota noch tro al dia.
Era no.us platz mos chans hi ma paria,
30 et ades sera l'alba!

Of dubious authenticity is the lover's answer which follows:

VII. Bel dous companh, tan sui en ric sojorn
qu'eu no volgra mais fos alba ni jorn,
car la gensor que anc nasques dè maire
tenc e abras, per qu'eu non prezi gaire
35 lo´ fol gilos ni l'alba.

Reis glorios, verais lums e clartatz, Deus poderos, Senher, si a vos platz, al meu companh siatz fizels aiuda; qu'eu no lo vi, pos la nochs fo venguda, et ades sera l'alba! 'Almighty God, true light and beacon, powerful Lord, if it pleases you, offer your precious help to my friend; for I have not seen him, since night fell, and soon dawn will come!'

Reis, Deus, Senher are all nominatives functioning as vocatives. The apposition to *Reis glorios, verais lums e clartatz,* is, of course, also in the nominative case.

verais < * *veracus*. CL *vēru* > *ver* and Old Fr. *veir, voir*. The Vulgar Latin of Gaul had created a form, * *veracu*, probably as a reinforcement of *vēru*; this same need for emphasis or additional phonetic substance is evident also in Sp. *verdadero*. The feminine form is *veraia*; the adjective agrees grammatically only with the first of two coordinated nouns.

lums < *lūmen* + *s*. Final *n* was lost in Vulgar Latin except in monosyllables: CL *nōmen* > VL *nome*; CL *lūmen* > VL *lume*.

poderos comes from *pŏtēre* > *poder* + the suffix *-ōsu* > *-os*; the same formation exists in Sp. Pg. *poderoso*.

companh - companho. It is puzzling to find *companh* used as an accusative, whereas *companho* appears as a nominative in the apostrophe that opens each stanza, with the sole exception of the lover's answer which reads *bel dous companh*. The regular declension of this imparisyllabic noun in Provençal is: nom. sing. *companh* or *companhs* (< * *companio*); acc. sing. *companhó* (< * *companiōne*); nom. plur. *companhó* (< * *companiōni*); acc. plur. *companhós* (< * *companiōnes*). The language of the troubadours shows a strong tendency to assimilate the imparisyllabic flexion into the most common masculine declension, that of *murs - mur*; it is a first step in that direction that leads to the alternance of forms with or without *s*, modeled on *murs - mur, mur - murs*, through the addition of an *s* in the nom. sing.: *companhs, bars* (< * *baro*), as well as through the creation, in Vulgar Latin, of a nom. plur. in *-i*: CL nom. and acc. plur. *homines* gives a VL nom. plur. *homini* and acc. plur. *homines*. Provençal seems to carry this process much further than does French, inasmuch as it draws new nominatives from the acusative, again by adding an *s*: the acc. *senhor* gives us a new nom. *senhors* for *senher*: *baró* yields a nom. *barós* for *bar*, etc. It would seem that only a general confusion between these two types of noun flexion and a beginning break-down of the declension system as a whole can help explain the rather unorthodox use of *companh* and *companhó* in this poem. The troubadour biographies contain examples of *los compans* and *los companhos* used as nominatives: *los compans demanderon l'alberc del borzes* (Boutière, p. 5, 14-15); *e.ls companhos colqueron lo en un bel lieg* (ib., p. 5, 19-20). It should further be pointed out that the use of the accusative as a direct address form is by no means uncommon, as seen from this example: *e tornet dir a sa mainada*: *Baros, yeu ai vist lo trachor* (Appel: Chr., 5, 326-327).

fizels < *fĭdēlis* is found in rhyme with *sagęl*, which seems to indicate a pronunciation with open *e*, probably under the influence of the very common *-ĕllu* suffix. The fluctuation in the development of intervocalic *d* gives us the variants *fidel* and *fiel*, of which the latter appears as early as the *Boeci*. The treatment of *ĭ* is learned.

aiuda. The frequentative type verb *adiutare*, simplified to *aiutare*, gives *aidar* (cf. Fr. *aider*) with loss of the intertonic vowel *u*. However, in other forms of this verb, *u* carried the main stress and was consequently kept as *u* [*y*]: *aiútat* > *ajuda*; an analogy with such forms leads to the creation of a new infinitive *ajudar* and the noun *ajuda* which has, beside it *aida*. Compare the Old French conjugation *aju - aidier*, and Old It. *aiuto - aitiamo*. [102]

---

[102] Cf. Rohlfs: Hist. Gr., § 538; Nyrop. vol. 2, §§ 16-17; and Fouché: Verbe, § 6.

nochs < *nŏctis for CL *nŏx*. The collateral development of *ct* to *it* gives *noit* < *nŏcte*, and both results may, of course, show conditioned diphthongization under the influence of the palatal: *nuoch, nuech, nuoit, nueit*.

venguda. CL *ventum* is replaced, in Vulgar Latin, by an *-ūtu* participle which, for Provençal, utilizes the root of the perfect.

Bel companho, si dormetz o velhatz, no dormatz plus, suau vos ressidatz; qu'en orien vei l'estela creguda d'amena.l jorn, qu'eu·l'ai be conoguda, et ades sera l'alba! 'My dear friend, whether you sleep or are awake, do not sleep any more, but wake up very gently; for in the East, I see the star looming which brings the day, I have recognized it, and soon dawn will come!'

velhatz < *vĭgĭlātis*. The *g'l* cluster gives a palatalized *l*, just like in Fr. *veillez*.

no dormatz plus. The subjunctive is quite frequently used with the value of an imperative: *digas li* 'tell him,' and this is particularly common in a negated context: *no m'oblidetz mia* 'do not forget me,' a familiar construction in Spanish syntax: *no durmáis más, no llores*.

suau < *sŭave*. The *u* achieves syllabicity when following an *s*; *suau* and Old Fr. *soef* thus count two syllables, as opposed to a non-syllabic *u* in Latin: *sŭa-ve*. Appel treats *suau* as a learned word with retention of the hiatus. Another feature that points to a learned influence is the continuation of *ŭ* as [y], yet the form *soau* is equally common, and the vocalization of final *v* is popular. The neuter form of several adjectives: *aut, bas, clar, dur, gen, leu, suau*, etc., may be used in adverbial function: *parla bas, eu chant clar, vola leu, se.n va tot ien e suau*. One example was found of *gens* used instead of the proper neuter form *gen*: *e fo ... gens parlans* (Boutière, p. 264, 2-4); this *s*, no doubt, reflects the characteristic adverbial ending.

ressidatz. CL *excĭtare* underwent influence of *cītus* for *cĭtus*, becoming *excītare > *eissidar*, or else the *i* is simply a learned feature. The verb was frequently reinforced by the prefixes *re-* or *de-*, yielding, in Provençal, *reissidar* and *desidar* (compare Tuscan *destare* and Emilian *resedarse*). A simplification of the diphthong *ei* to *e* occurs frequently in the pretonic position: *reissidar* > *ressidar*. [103]

creguda. The Classical Latin perfect *crēvī* became, in Vulgar Latin, * *crevui* which gives *cric;* the past participle *cregut* is based on this root in its non-*umlaut* form (cf. *crec* < * *crevuit*). In the same fashion, *co(g)nōvī* becomes * *conovui* > *conoc* (instead of the extremely rare *umlaut* form *conuc*), and we get the past participle *conogut*.

Bel companho, en chantan vos appel; no dormatz plus, qu'eu auch chantar l'auzel que vai queren lo jorn per lo boschatge et ai paor que.l gilos vos assatge, et ades sera l'alba! 'My dear friend, I am calling you with my song; do not sleep any more, for I hear the bird sing that is searching for daylight in the forest, and I am afraid that the jealous man may surprise you, and soon dawn will come!'

auch < *audio*. Final *di̯* gives a sound which was, no doubt, the voiceless [*tš*], although the spelling is most often *-g*: *aug, gaug* (< *gaudiu*), *rag* (< *radiu*). This graph may originally have representend an earlier voiced stage of the development. Voiced final plosives constitute one of the most striking archaic features of *la Sainte Foi d'Agen*: *jag* (< *iacuit*), *preg* (from *pregar*), *cab* (< *capu* < CL *caput*), *-ad, -id* (< *-ātu, -ītu*), which goes to prove that intervocalic voicing precedes the loss of the final vowel in Provençal.

auzel < *aucĕllu*. Intervocalically, *k* before *e, i* gives a voiced *s* via a transitional affricate stage [*dz*] which may be inferred from the change of final prepalatal *k* to [*ts*]: *vōce* > *votz*; *vĭce* > *vetz*. Other examples of intervocalic prepalatal *k*: *placēre* > *plazer*; CL *vīcīnu* > VL *vecīnu > *vezi*; CL *coquīna* > VL *cocīna

---

[103] Cf. REW 2970 *excĭtāre*; and FEW, art. *excĭtāre*.

> *cozina*. For *auzel*, Provençal has an alternate form, *aucel*, explained by Appel (§ 46a) as resulting from the lack of a true intervocalic condition after *au* (compare Sp. *poco* < *paucu*), and he gives examples of the retention of *k* before *a* in that position: *auca, pauca*, yet *au* does not always constitute a barrier to voicing in Provençal: *auzar, cauza*. To Crescini (pps. 32-33), oscillations in graph: *auzel, aussella, aucellayre*, furnish proof that prepalatal *k* may lead to either a voiced or a voiceless result in intervocalic position. While graphic fluctuations are, indeed, prevalent in Provençal for the notation of affricates as well as for voiced and voiceless *s*: *Proenza, Proenssa, Proensa*; *proeza, proesa, proessa*, etc., it is not easy to justify a voiceless outcome in intervocalic position on that sole criterion. Appel's explanation thus remains the more plausible of the two, if one may not simply assess *aucel* as a case of learned spelling.

boschatge is a derivation from Frankish * *bŭsk* > *bosc*, combined with the *-aticu* suffix; cf. Old Fr. *boscage*, Fr. *bocage*. The *ch* spelling indicates palatalization of *c* before *a*.

gilos < *zelōsu*. In this early borrowing from Greek, initial *z* was treated like the *dį*- cluster (cf. *diŭrnu* > *jorn*, and compare also Fr. *jaloux*), whereas more recent loan-words from Greek continue initial *z* as a voiced *s*: *zel*, Fr. *zèle* < *zelu*. The initial palatal causes the closure of pretonic *e* to *i*; other examples of this trend are: *ginolh* < *genŭcŭlu*; *Giraut* < *Gêrald*; *gilar* < *gĕlare*. In French *jaloux*, the opening of *e* to *a* is produced by the following *l*; Provençal examples of this feature are: *delphūnu* > *dalfin*; *eleemosyna* > *almosina* > *almosna, almorna*.

assatge is the pres. subj. of *assajar* 'to test, try, attack,' a verb derived from *essai, assai, ensai* < *exagiu*. The prefix *es-* is often reinforced to *as-* or *en-* as seen above (compare also It. *assaggiare* and Sp. *ensayar*), and it may even be dropped (cf. It. *saggio*). Originally, *exagium* meant 'weight, weighing,' but it is attested, from the fourth century on, with the meaning 'attempt, try' which is continued in Romance. [104]

---

[104] Cf. FEW, art. *exagium*. Hamlin (28, 14) derives *assatge* from *assetjar* 'to besiege', but does not explain why we then would have *assatge* instead of *assetge*.

Bel companho, issetz al fenestrel e regardatz las estelas del cel! Conoisseretz si.us sui fizels messatge; si non o faitz, vostres n'er lo damnatge, et ades sera l'alba! 'My dear friend, go to the window and look at the stars in the sky! And you will realize that I have served you as a faithful messenger; if you do not, you will suffer the consequences, and soon dawn will come!'

issetz. *Exītis* gives *eissetz* or *issetz* with the traditional reduction of pretonic *ei* to *i*. The Classical Latin plural imperative does not survive in Gallo-Romance, where its functions are assumed by the 2. pers. plur. of the pres. ind.: *cantātis, vĭdētis, vendĭtis* > Pr. *cantatz, vezętz, vendętz* and Fr. *chantez, voyez, vendez,* as opposed to Sp. *cantad, ved, vended* which continue the Latin imperatives *cantāte, vĭdēte, vendĭte.* The first conjugation ending, *-atz* < *-ātis,* is phonological, but the remaining three conjugation endings, *-ētis, -ĭtis* and *-ītis,* all go to *-ętz* with an open *e* stemming from an analogy with *ętz* < *ĕstis,* instead of a phonological **-ętz* and **-itz* (*crĕdĭtis* had become VL *credétis* in an effort to level out the stress difference of the *-ĕre* conjugation).[105]

fenestrel. As a diminutive of *fenestra,* Provençal has both a masc. *fenestrel* and a fem. *fenestrela,* based on the *-ĕllu/-ĕlla* suffix. Similar diminutives obtain for *porta*: *portel* and *portela.* The final *a* is dropped when the suffix is added; cf. *(a)laud(a)* + *-ĭtta* > *lauzeta.*

messatge lacks a flexional *s,* as is the case also of *damnatge,* subject of the verb *er* (< *ĕrit*).

faitz < *facĭtis* is the 2. pers. plur. of the pres. ind. This very common verb has kept its Classical Latin accentuation (compare *crĕdĭtis* > VL *crēdĕtis > *crezetz*) in its phonological development in Gallo-Romance: Pr. *faitz,* Fr. *faites.* In the same manner, *facĭmus* gives *faim* and Old Fr. *faimes,* but we also find analogical formations in Provençal, showing the normal stressed endings *-em* and *-etz*: *fazém, fazétz* (cf. Fr. *faisons* which has completely ousted

---

[105] See Lausberg, §§ 805, 869, 872, 879 and 886. Spanish maintains a clear distinction between the imperative and the pres. ind.: *cantāte* > *cantad*; *cantātis* > *cantáis.*

Old Fr. *faimes*, whereas *faites* is kept). Compare the verb *dīcĭmus - dīcĭtis* > *dizem, dizetz*, with only rare cases of *ditz* and no stem-stressed form from *dīcĭmus*. The most common form of *faire* in the 1. pers. plur. of the pres. ind. is *fam*, drawn from an analogy with *dam* (< *dāmus*) and *estam* (< *stamus*).

vostres. CL *vester* was changed to *voster* under the influence of *noster*; it carries an analogical flexional *s* of the nom. sing.

Bel companho, pos me parti de vos, eu no.m dormi ni.m moc de genolhos, ans preiei Deu, lo filh Santa Maria, que.us me rendes per leial companhia, et ades sera l'alba! 'My dear friend, since I left you, I have not slept nor have I ceased to kneel down, praying God, the Son of the Virgin Mary, to bring my loyal friend back to me, and soon dawn will come!'

parti < *partii*. Classical Latin admitted both *partii* and *partīvi* in agreement with a phonological rule to the effect that *v* could drop between identical vowels (cf. * *vivita* > CL *vīta*). Only the form *partii* is continued in Gallo-Romance, and it is by analogy with *-ii* that the first conjugation perfect ending *-avit* is reduced to *-a* in Provençal: *perseverá, mená, mandá*, etc.

.m dormi. Intransitive verbs are often used reflexively in the old language; cf. *me parti de vos*, and, for Old French, *Karles se dort*, in the *Chanson de Roland*.

moc < VL * *movui* < CL *mōvī*. One might have expected * *muc* under the influence of final long *i*, but no such form has been attested. For *conoc* (< VL * *conovui* < CL *co(g)nōvī*), on the other hand, my readings yielded one example of *conuc*: *anc no fo q'eu estes ses desir, pos vos conuc* (Boutière, p. 324, 10-11), and Crescini gives an example of it in rhyme, quoted from Erdmannsdörfer; it is, no doubt, a very rare occurrence. [106]

genolhos. Adverbs in *-ons* (*-os*) are little used in Gallo-Romance and are kept, in modern French, only in two expressions: *à reculons*

---

[106] Cf. Crescini, p. 119.

and *à tâtons*. Old French had a few more of these constructions which all appear to deal with a particular position of the body: *a genouillons, a ventrillons, a chevauchons* (Pr. *de cavalcons*), *a cropeton*. Provençal uses the preposition *de* in this construction: *pueys si gieton de ginolhos* (*La Vie de sainte Enimie*, v. 1566), but there are cases of *a* like in French: *gietan s'a genolhos* (Appel), 7,18). The origin of this adverbial suffix is yet to be fully elucidated. It is perhaps somewhat more frequent in Italian (*-oni*): *bocconi, ginocchioni, penzoloni*, but is virtually unknown outside of Gallo- and Italo-Romance. [107]

lo filh Santa Maria. With words designating persons, the genitive function may be expressed through the simple juxtaposition of two nouns the second of which, denoting the possessor, is always in the accusative; no preposition is used. This is a very common construction in Old French as well: *la niece le duc* 'the duke's niece.' A different word order obtains, in both languages, with short words like *deu, dieu*: *la Deu beneïzo* 'God's blessing'; and an example from Old French: *li deo inimi* 'God's enemies.' This word order, however, is not compulsory: *per amor dieu* (Appel: Chr., 5, 367), as compared with *pro deo amur* in the *Serments de Strasbourg*.

rendes < **rendĕdĭsset*. Etymologically, the imperfect subjunctive continues the Latin pluperfect subjunctive; its characteristic vowel ę comes from the *-ęi* perfect. Lausberg points to the fact that **dĕïsse*, obtained from CL *dĕdĭssem* through consonantal dissimilation, could resolve its *ĕï* hiatus either as *ĭ*: **dĭsse* > It. *dęsse*, or as *ĕ*: **dĕsse* > Pr. *dęs*, Sp. *diese*, Pg. *dęsse*. [108]

leial < *lēgāle*. The development of *g* before *a* inside a word is not uniform; it is either kept or it becomes a yod which, in some regions, is pronounced [dž]: *nĕgāre* > *negar, neiar, nejar*. Grandgent attempts a dialectal distribution of the three results, but no plausible explanation has as yet been offered of this variety. The

---

[107] Cf. Nyrop, vol. 3, §§ 600-602. Silvio Pieri discusses the origin of It. *-one, -oni*, in *Romania*, vol. 33, 1904, pps. 230-238; and in *ZRPh*, vol. 30, 1906, pps. 337-339.

[108] Cf. Lausberg, § 829; and Crescini, p. 121.

two adjectives, *lēgāle* and *rēgāle*, show the developments to yod and [dž], but *g* is never kept; on the contrary, a complete loss of *g* is quite common: *lēgāle* > *leyal, lejal, leal* and also *lial* (with raising of *e* in hiatus). French has *loyal* and *royal*, but also the rarer form *réal* (as in *Montréal*) which Nyrop seems to consider a Spanish borrowing. In view of its common occurrence in Provençal, it seems perfectly legitimate, however, to consider it a genuine Gallo-Romance development. [109]

Bel companho, la foras als peiros me preiavatz qu'eu no fos dormilhos, enans velhes tota noch tro al dia. Era no.us platz mos chans ni ma paria, et ades sera l'alba! 'My dear friend, out there on the front steps, you asked me not to go to sleep, but rather to stay awake all night until dawn. And now, neither my song nor my company pleases you. And soon dawn will come!'

foras. Classical Latin had both *fŏris* and *fŏras*, continued in Provençal as *fors* and *foras* (*fora*). For Fr. *fors*, von Wartburg rightly points out that, in view of the proclitic nature of the word, it is not possible to decide whether it continues *fŏris* or *fŏras*. It would seem plausible, for Provençal, that the alternance between *fors* and *foras* could explain the unusual ocurrence of *senas* in the deeds for *ses* (< *sĭne* + *s*); the origin of this form is obscure and has been much debated, but no definite solution has as yet been found. Grafström concludes his examination by stating that "le débat n'est donc toujours pas clos." [110]

peiros < *pĕtrōnes*, with the normal development of *tr* to *i̯r* and an unstable *n* before flexional *s*.

dormilhos is derived from the verb *dŏrmīcŭlāre* through the addition of the *-ōsu* suffix to the stem. Old French has *dormillous*, Spanish has *dormijoso*.

enans < *ĭn-ante* + *s*. *Inante*, formed like *abante*, is found in the *Peregrinatio Aetheriæ ad Loca Sancta*; in Gallo-Romance, it is

---

[109] Cf. Grandgent, § 65; and Nyrop, vol. 2, § 295.
[110] Cf. Grafström: Morph., §§ 74-75; and FEW, art. *fŏrās*.

THE TROUBADOUR POETRY 125

encountered only in the Provençal linguistic domain, not in French. It also survives in such combinations as *denan, adenan, derenan*; Catalan has *enant* and *adenant*, and Spanish has *delante* with a consonantal dissimilation. [111]

enans velhes is a paratactic construction which depends logically on *preiavatz*, although there is no formal introduction by *que*.

tro is a weakened form of *entro* < *ĭnter hŏc*; the conjunction *entro que* could also be reinforced: *entro tant que* (the French parallel is *jusqu'à tant que*). [112]

era. Ha hōra or *hac hōra* are the etymologies suggested by Rohlfs for Fr. *or, ore* and Pr. *ara*: *ha hŏra* > *aora* > *aura* > *ore* and proclitic *or*. The etymology *ha hōra* seems preferable for Provençal, where the velar *c* of *hac hōra* would voice to *g*, but would not disappear (cf. *acūtu* > *agut*; *sĕcŭndu* > *segon*; and compare Old Sp. *agora* < *hac hōra*). The development of *ha hōra* to *a(o)ra* and *ara* is still not quite clear; we seem to have a reduction brought on by proclitic usage. The form *era* is equally unclear; Appel suggests *éa hora*, but not without some hesitation. One might add that a fluctuation between *ar* and *er* is widespread. The loss of the final vowel (*ar, er,* Fr. *or*) is due to the weak proclitic position. [113]

Bel dous companh, tan sui en ric sojorn qu'eu no volgra mais fos alba ni jorn, car la gensor que anc nasques de maire tenc e abras, per qu'eu non prezi gaire lo fol gilos ni l'alba. 'My dear friend, I am in such delightful company that I wish that daylight would never come, for I hold in my arms the most beautiful lady ever born, and therefore I do not care about the jealous fool nor about dawn.'

---

[111] Cf. FEW, art. *ĭnante*.
[112] Grafström (Morph., § 74) derives *tro* from an analogy with the many adverbs or prepositions which often appear with an added *en*: *aisi - enaisi; apres - enapres*. See also Rohlfs, p. 67 and note 134.
[113] See Rohlfs, p. 81 and note 189; FEW, art. *hōra*; and Appel, § 39. Depending on the stress, Appel has *há hora* > *ara* and *ha hóra* > *aora*. Grandgent (§ 33,3) derives *ara, era* from a Greek word *ara*, an etymology which was already suggested by Meyer-Lübke. For Old Sp. *agora*, see Menéndez Pidal, § 128, 3.

sojorn is a derivation of *sŭbdiŭrnāre* > *sojornar*; Provençal also has the dissimilated form *sejornar* (cf. Fr. *séjourner*).

volgra < *vŏlueram* is a second conditional.

gensor is an example of a synthetic Latin comparative which has been kept in Provençal. The postulated comparative of the adjective *gĕnĭtus* is * *gen(i)tior* > *génser* (nom.) and * *gen(i)tiōre* > *gensór* (acc.). Other survivals of synthetic comparatives in Provençal are: *mélher - melhór* (< *mĕlior - mĕliōre*), *peire - pejor* (< *pĕior - pĕiōre*), *menre - menor* (< *mĭnor - mĭnōre*), etc. [114]

nasques is the 3. pers. sing. of the imperfect subj. of *naisser* < VL *nascĕre* < CL *nascī*. The popular Latin language showed an early trend towards treating deponents as active verbs; Cato uses *nascĕre*, Plautus has *hortāre* for *hortārī*, and a Pompeian inscription carries *tutat* for *tutatur*. In Provençal, a weak perfect is formed from the stem *nasc-*: *nasquei, nasquest, nasquet*, and the same stem is used in the imperfect subj. *nasques* (cf. *cantęs, vendęs* with the stem and open *e* of *cantęi, vendęi*). The rare 3. pers. sing. perf. ind. *nasc* testifies to the existence, however fleeting, of an *-ui* perfect: * *nascuit*. The verb *iraisser* < VL * *irascĕre* < CL *irascī* is treated exactly like *naisser*. [115]

maire < *mātre*, with the cluster *tr* going to yod + *r*, followed by a supporting vowel.

tenc. *Tĕneo* gives regularly *tenh*; cf. *vĕnio* > *venh*; *remaneo* > *remanh*. A large group of Latin verbs in *-go* gave a *-c* ending through regular phonological development in Provençal: *frango* > *franc*; *plango* > *planc*; *stringo* > *estrenc*. Collateral forms in *-nh*

---

[114] Cf. Elcock, pps. 69-70; and Crescini, pps. 74-75. The exact etymology of *genser - gensor* is not quite clear; Elcock gives * *gĕnitior*, but does not explain how the stressed *i* is eliminated. * *Gĕnitiōre*, with an intertonic *i*, does, of course, not pose the same problem, and it is tempting to postulate an analogical * *gĕntior* from there for the nominative. Crescini avoids giving any Latin etymon and simply quotes *genser - gensor* as comparatives of the adjective *gent, gen*. Nyrop (vol. 2, § 454, 3) suggests an analogy with *fort - forzor*.

[115] For the treatment of deponents in Vulgar Latin, see Väänänen, § 294.

(*franh, planh, estrenh*), drawn from the infinitives *franher, planher, estrenher*, link this group of verbs with *venh, tenh, remanh* on which they exert a morphological pressure which eventually leads to the creation of *tenc, venc, remanc* (*planh - planc* gives us *tenh - x : tenc*). *Frangĕre > franher* represents the regular phonological outcome of intervocalic *ng* before a palatal vowel, whereas, placed before *o*, the final vowel will drop and *g* will desonorize. [116]

abras is the 1. pers. sing. of the pres. ind. of the verb *abrasar* (cf. Fr. *embrasser* with a different prefix, but Sp. *abrazar*), derived from *bratz < brachiu*. The neuter plural *brachia* is continued as *brassa*, Fr. *brasse*, Sp. *braza*, etc., a measure of length. The c_i cluster, when final, becomes *tz*: *brachiu > bratz*; *facio > fatz*; *glacie > glatz*. In intervocalic position, c_i originally became [*ts*] as shown by final c_i, but the [*ts*] affricate had evolved into a voiceless *s* already in preliterary times: *brachia > brassa*; *faciam > fassa*; *placeam > plassa*; and likewise when following a consonant: *bilancia > *balancia > balansa*; *dŭlcis > *dŭlcia > doussa*. Here, however, *z* is a rather common graph, reflecting the assibilated stage of the development: *dolzament, Proenza*, etc.

gaire. Germanic **waigaro* gives *gaigre* and *gaire* with retention of the Germanic diphthong *ai*. When initial *w*- becomes *g*, the original *g* may disappear through dissimilation. The two forms, *gaigre* and *gaire*, could also reflect learned versus popular treatment of the *g'r* cluster: retention in *gaigre*, change to *ir* with the yod absorbed by the preceding diphthong in *gaire*. Cf. *nĭgru > neir* or *negre*; CL *íntĕgru >* VL *íntĕgru > entier, entieir* or *entegre*.

---

[116] A close parallel to this whole development exists in Italian where older *tegno, vegno, rimagno* yield to *tengo, vengo, rimango*. Cf. Rohlfs: Hist. Gr., § 535. Spanish shows a similar change to *-go*: *tengo, vengo*, while Portuguese retains the palatalized stage: *tenho, venho*. Cf. Menéndez Pidal, § 113, 2, b.

BIBLIOGRAPHY

Anglade, J. *Grammaire de l'Ancien Provençal.* Paris: Klincksieck, 1921.
Anglade, J. *Les Poésies de Peire Vidal.* Paris: Champion, 1923.
Anglade, J. *Les Troubadours.* Paris: A. Colin, 1929.
Appel, C. *Provenzalische Chrestomathie.* Leipzig: Reisland, 1930.
Appel, C. *Provenzalische Lautlehre.* Leipzig: Reisland, 1918.
Badía Margarit, A. *Gramática histórica catalana.* Barcelona: Editorial Noguer, 1951.
Bec, P. *La Langue occitane.* Paris, 1963.
Bertoni, G. *Italia dialettale.* Milano, 1916.
Bourciez, Ed. *Éléments de Linguistique romane.* Paris: Klincksieck, 1956.
Boutière, J., and Schutz, A.-H. *Biographies des Troubadours.* Paris-Toulouse, 1950.
Brunel, C. *Les plus anciennes Chartes en Langue provençale.* Paris, 1926, 1952.
La Chanson de Sainte Foi d'Agen, edited by A. Thomas. Paris: Champion, 1925.
Corominas, J. *Diccionario crítico etimológico de la lengua castellana.* Madrid, 1954-57.
Crescini, V. *Manuale per l'avviamento agli studi provenzali.* Milano: Hoepli, 1926.
Elcock, W. D. *The Romance Languages.* London: Faber and Faber, 1960.
Fouché, P. *Morphologie historique du Français. Le Verbe.* Paris: Klincksieck, 1967.
Fouché, P. *Phonétique historique du Français.* Paris, 1953-58.
Foulet, L. *Petite Syntaxe de l'Ancien Français.* Paris: Champion, 1968.
Gamillscheg, E. *Romania germanica.* Berlin, 1934-36.
Grafström, Å. *Étude sur la Graphie des plus anciennes Chartes languedociennes.* Uppsala: Almqvist, 1958.
Grafström, Å. *Étude sur la Morphologie des plus anciennes Chartes languedociennes.* Uppsala: Almqvist, 1968.
Grandgent, C. H. *An Outline of the Phonology and Morphology of Old Provençal.* Boston: Heath, 1905.
Hamlin, F., Ricketts, P. T., and Hathaway, J. *Introduction à l'Étude de l'Ancien Provençal.* Genève: Droz, 1967.
Hoepffner, E. *Les Troubadours.* Paris: A. Colin, 1955.
Jeanroy, A. *La Poésie lyrique des Troubadours.* Toulouse - Paris, 1934.
Kuhn, A. *Romanische Philologie.* Berne: Francke Verlag, 1951.

Lausberg, H. *Romanische Sprachwissenschaft.* Berlin: W. de Gruyter, 1958-62.
Lévy, E. *Petit Dictionnaire provençal-français.* Heidelberg: Winter, 1966.
Lévy, E. *Provenzalisches Supplement-Wörterbuch.* Leipzig, 1894-1924.
Malkiel, Y. *Linguistica Generale Filologia Romanza Etimologia.* Firenze: Sansoni, 1970.
Menéndez Pidal, R. *Manual de gramática histórica española.* Madrid: Espasa-Calpe, 1952.
Meyer-Lübke, W. *Das Katalanische.* Heidelberg: Winter, 1925.
Meyer-Lübke, W. *Romanisches etymologisches Wörterbuch.* Heidelberg: Winter, 1935.
Millardet, G. *Linguistique et Dialectologie romanes.* Paris: Champion, 1923.
Moll y Casasnovas, F. de B. *Gramática histórica catalana.* Madrid: Gredos, 1952.
Monteverdi, A. *Manuale d'avviamento agli studi romanzi.* Milano: Vallardi, 1952.
Nyrop, Kr. *Grammaire historique de la Langue française.* Copenhagen: Gyldendal, 1924-30.
Pfister, M. *—PS— in den romanischen Sprachen.* Berne, 1960.
Pillet, A., and Carstens, H. *Bibliographie des Troubadours.* Halle: Niemeyer, 1933.
Rémy, P. *La Littérature provençale au Moyen Age.* Bruxelles, 1944.
Rheinfelder, H. *Altfranzösische Grammatik.* München: Max Hüber Verlag, 1963, 1967.
Richter, E. *Beiträge zur Geschichte der Romanismen.* Halle, 1934.
Riquer, M. de. *La lírica de los trovadores.* Barcelona, 1948.
Rohlfs, G. *Einführung in das Studium der romanischen Philologie.* Heidelberg: Winter, 1966.
Rohlfs, G. *Historische Grammatik der Italienischen Sprache.* Berne: Francke Verlag, 1954.
Rohlfs, G. *Le Gascon, Études de Philologie pyrénéenne.* Halle, 1935.
Rohlfs, G. *Romanische Philologie.* Heidelberg: Winter, 1950-52.
Rohlfs, G. *Sermo Vulgaris Latinus.* Halle: Niemeyer, 1951.
Rohlfs, G. *Vom Vulgärlatein zum Altfranzösischen.* Tübingen: Niemeyer, 1960.
Roncaglia, A. *La lingua dei Trovatori.* Roma: Ateneo, 1965.
Ronjat, J. *Grammaire historique des Parlers provençaux modernes.* Montpellier, 1930-1941.
Schultz-Gora, O. *Altprovenzalisches Elementarbuch.* Heidelberg: Winter, 1936.
Stimming, A. *Bertran von Born.* Halle: Niemeyer, 1892.
Stolz, F., and Debrunner, A., and Schmid, W. P. *Geschichte der lateinischen Sprache.* Berlin: W. de Gruyter, 1966.
Strónski, S. *Le Troubadour Folquet de Marseille.* Krakow, 1910.
Tagliavini, C. *Le Origini delle lingue neolatine.* Bologna: Pàtron, 1964.
Väänänen, V. *Introduction au Latin vulgaire.* Paris: Klincksieck, 1963.
Vàrvaro, A. *Linguistica romanza.* Napoli, 1968.
Vidos, B. E. *Manual de lingüística románica.* Madrid: Aguilar, 1963.
Wartburg, W. von. *Französisches etymologisches Wörterbuch.* Bonn - Leipzig - Basel, 1922 ff.
Williams, E. B. *From Latin to Portuguese.* Philadelphia, 1962.

Articles Quoted

F. Bergert, "Die von den Trobadors genannten oder gefeierten Damen," in *ZRPh*, Beiheft 46, Halle, 1913.

A. Jeanroy, "Les Biographies des Troubadours," in *AR*, vol. 1, 1917, p. 289 ff.

P. Meyer, "*C* et *G* suivis d'*A* en provençal," in *Romania*, vol. 24, 1895, pps. 529-575, and vol. 30, 1901, pps. 393-398.

G. Millardet, "A propos de provençal *dins*," in *RLR*, vol. 57, 1914, pps. 189-203.

M. Pfister, "Beiträge zur altprovenzalischen Grammatik," in *Vox Romanica*, vol. 17, 1958, pps. 281-362.

M. Pfister, "Beiträge zur altprovenzalischen Lexikologie," in *Vox Romanica*, vol. 18, 1959, pps. 220-296.

Silvio Pieri, "Il tipo avverbiale di *carpone, -i*," in *Romania*, vol. 33, 1904, pps. 230-238.

Silvio Pieri, "Il tipo avverbiale di *carpone, -i*," in *ZRPh*, vol. 30, 1906, pps. 337-339.

E. Richter, "Die Aussprache des [*u*] im Altprovenzalischen," in *ZRPh*, vol. 45, 1925-1926, pps. 385-401.

E. Richter, "Zu prov. *En* = Herr. Prov.-katal. *a-n-el*," in *ZRPh*, vol. 27, 1903, pps. 193-197.

E. Richter, "Zur *u - ü* - Frage," in *ZRPh*, vol. 41, 1921, pps. 88-95.

F. Schürr, "Diphtongaison romane," in *Revue de linguistique romane*, vol. 20, pps. 107 and 161.

F. Schürr, "Nochmals über Umlaut und Diphthongierung in der Romania," in *RF*, vol. 52, pps. 311-318.

F. Schürr, "Umlaut und Diphthongierung in der Romania," in *RF*, vol. 50, pps. 275-316.

A. Thomas, "*En* et *na* en provençal," in *Romania*, vol. 12, 1883, pps. 585-587.

A Thomas, "Le Nominatif pluriel asymétrique des substantifs masculins en ancien provençal," in *Romania*, vol. 34, 1905, pps. 353-363.

WORD INDEX

References are to pages or to footnotes. Old, modern and dialectal forms are all subsumed under the same language heading.

Provençal

a 47
ab 29
abrasar 127
ac 28, 36, 37, 65, 88, 94, n. 27
acolhir 108
acuoilla 108
ad 47
-ad 119
adenan 124
ades 38
agra 95
agron 74
aguda 61
agues 57
agueron 74
aguessen 36
agui 88, 94
aguist 65
agut (< acutu) 125
agut (< *habutu) 60, 71
ai 63, 85
aic 88
aicel 113
aicest 113
aida 117
aidar 117
aise 110, n. 97
aissi 89, n. 112
aissina n. 97
aital 113
aitan 113
aitz 110, n. 97
aizina 110, n. 97

aizinar n. 97
ajuda 117
alba 59
albergar 59
alegres 58
almorna 120
almos(i)na 120
-alh 44
als 42
alt 59
am 29
amach 76
amag 76
amb 29
amia 103
amiga 20, 103
an (cf. ab) 29
an 113
anar 49, n. 49
anc 73
ancar 73
ancse(n) 85
ancsempre 85
anet 48
anz 106, n. 77
aon 96
aora n. 113
ap 29
apres 38, n. 112
aquel(s) 44
aquest 75
ar(a) 125, n. 113
as- 120
assai 120
assajar 120

assatge 120, n. 104
asses 55
assis 55
ataïnar n. 98
atayna 110
-atge 111, n. 99
-atgue n. 99
-atje 111
atretals 92
au(n) 113
aucel 120
auch 83, 119
aug 83, 119
aur 19
aurai 87
aussella 120
aut 58, 59
autra 59
autrui 45
auzar 84
auzel 119
auzir 20
aven 64
avenen 105
aver 19
avetz 75
avia 27
avinen 105
avut 60, 71
az 47, 67, 87, 106
azori 91

balansa 127
Balaidsvila n. 53
Balazvila n. 53

INDEX

bar 41
baro(n) 41
bars, 41, 117
baros 117
be(n) 26
belazor 51
beltat 59, 104
beltatz 104
beutat 59
bisbe 26, n. 14
bispe 26
borc 74
borges 45, 74
borzes 45
boschatge 120
brassa 127
bratz 127
br(i)eu 43
breujar 62

cab 119
cabelh 76
cabra 19
caire 20
caissa 87
c(h)aitiu 96
calt 59
c(h)an (< cantem) 106
can(t) (< canto) n. 80
can(t) (< quando) 31, 58, n. 100
can(t) (< quantu) 31
cantada 61
cantador 33
cantaire 33
cantan (< cantant) 42, 60
cantan (< cantante) 64
cantara 94
cantarai 95
cantaras 95
cantarem 95
cantaretz 95
cantat 60
cantatz 121
cantava 34
canten 42
cantera 94
canteron 74
cantet 65, 77
canton 42, 60
cap 21, 29

captenemen 90
c(h)aptener 90
captenensa 90
captenh 90
car 31
carcer 20, 104
cargar 48
c(h)arjar 48
c(h)ascus 34
cassar 39
caseguda 71
casse(r) 20, 104
c(h)astelas 26
caut 59
caval 34
cavalcons 123
cavalgar 59
cavalh 44
c(h)avaliers 32
cazec 68, 71, 93
cazeguts 93
c(h)azer 93
cazet 68, 71, 93
c(h)zaut 71, 93
cela 94
cel(s) 44
celei(s) 86
cest 44
cesta 94
cellui 45
cilh 94, 97
cinc 68
cist 94, 97
clau 20, 43
coa 75
cobde 91
cobre 105
cobri 105
cofon 91
c(u)olh 108
colp 60
com(a) 39
companh(s) 116, 117
companhó(s) 116, 117
coms 30
comte 30
confortar 105
conoc 119, 122
conogut 119
conoisser 104
conortar 105
conosc 86

conquerir 51
conquerre 51
conques 55
conquest 52
conquis 55
conquistar 52
conselh 37
consirar 77
consiros 77
conuc 119, 122
cop 60
cors 108
corses 35
cosel 36
cosselh 37
cossiros 77
covenir 91
cozina 120
cre(i) 63
crec 119
creguda 119
cregut 119
creire 20
creisser 20
crezia 34, 42
cric 119
crida 66
cru 63
cru(d)el 90
cruzel 90
cu(i)da 36
cuelh 108
cuidar 86
cuidava 86
cui 59, 85
cujar 57
cum 89
Cypry 46, 50

da(i) 92
dalfin 120
dam 68
dan (< damnu) 68
dan (< dant) 113
dans 68
dat 47
dau 92
de n. 94
dec 37
ded 77
dedins 55
defendre 89

degra 94
dels 42
denan 124
dens 55
dentz 55
derenan 124
des 123
des(s)e 85
desempre 85
desidar 119
desiritar 57
desplai 109
desplatz 109
destrui 90
det 77
deu 92
d(i)eu 19, 29, 43
deude 91
deute 91
devinar 30
dezirar 86
dezir(i)er, 86
dia 64
di(g)a 103
dic 91
dich 62
dig 55, 62
dijous 64
dins 55
dinz 55
dir(e) 45
dis (< dixi) 55
dis (< dixit) 45
dit 55, 62
ditz 122
divenres 64
dizem 122
dizen 64
dizetz 122
do(n) n. 80
dolc 37
dolza 84
dombredieus 109
dom(i)na 89
domnejar 33
domnejaire 33
dompna 90
dompnidieus 109
don 75
dona 89
donada 47
donas n. 80

donava 47
doptar 91
dopte 91
dormilhos 124
dormon 60
dous(s)a 84, 127
doussor 84
dreihz 97
drutz 47
dui n. 73
duoilla 108
dutz n. 73

e(t) 67
edificis 56
ef(f)ant n. 79
e(n)fan 91
eissam 98
eisselh 97
eissetz 121
eissidar 118
eissilh 97
eissir 98
el (< en + lo) 110
el (< ille, illu) 36, 63, 67
el (< illud) 63
el(l)a 50, 94
elh 36, 37
-elh 44
elhs 67
els 67
empararitz 52
emperador 33, 52
emperaire 33, 52
emperairitz 52
emperi 46
En 47, 48
en- 120
enaissi 89, n. 112
enans 124
enapres n. 112
enganada 104
engan 104
enjan 104
enjanar 104
ens 55
ensai 120
ensemble n. 31
ensems 36, 37
ensenhar 37
entegre 127

entendement 105
entendimen 105
ent(i)eir 127
entro 125
entz 55
enueg 83
enueitz 83
enveya 84
enviar 77
enviet 77
-(i)er 32
er (< erit) 102, 121
er(a) 125, n. 113
era (< erat) 34
eram 35
eratz 35
eravam 35
eravatz 35
eretar 57
eretat 57
eritar 57
es (< est) 70
es (< estis) 70
escola 21
escombatre 77
esdeve(n) 93
esdevenir 77
esgardar 77
esperjuret 77
espiar n. 90
espina 21, 66
essai 120
essems 36, 37
essenhar 37
esser 104
est 70
esta(i) 92
estan 113
estar 21
estau 92
estrenc 126
estrenh 126
estrenher 126
-eta 83
etz 70, 107
eu 85, 97
eus n. 60
evesc(h)at 26
evesque 26
ez 67, 87, 106

fa 92

INDEX

fach 34, 93, 97
fag 69, 93, 97
fah 97
fai 91, 92, n. 73
faich 97
faicha 57
faih 93, 97
faillitz 63
faim 121
faire 39
fait 34, 69
faita 57
faitz 121
falhir 63
falhitz 63
fals 59
familha n. 88
far 39
fassa 127
fatz 84, 127
fazem 121
fazetz 121
faus 59
fava 34, 76
fe n. 94
feble 92
femna 89
fenestrel(a) 121
fenir 30
fenna 89
ferian 60
ferion 60
fetz 106, n. 94
fi 105, n. 94
fi(z)ar 90
fi(d)el 117
Figa(i)ret n. 53
fil(h)s 37, 42
filz 42
fina 111
finimen 105
fis (< feci) 105, n. 94
fis (< finis) 111
fizels 117
fluvi 33, 46
fo(n) 26, 28, 61
folher 45
folh(a) 56
folias 44, 47
folzer 45, 109
fom 26
fon (< fonte) 89

fon (< fundit) 86
fora 95
fora(s) 124
foron 26
fors 124
forsa 38, 50
forsenar 62
fort n. 114
forza 38, 50
fos 42
fossen 42
fosson 42
fotz 26
fouzer 109
frachura 34
fra(i)del n. 53
fraire 30, 37
fraitura 34
franc 126
francs 107
franh 126
franher 126
Fransa 38
Franza 37, 38
frire 59
fui (< fui) 26
fui (<fugit) 90
fulias 44, 47
fust 26

gai(g)re 127
gal 21
g(r)anre 74
garir 48
garritz 48
gauch 83
gaug 83, 119
gauzir 85
gazaingnar 51
gen 61
gen(t) n. 114
genolhos 122
gens 112
genser 126, n. 114
gensor 126, n. 114
gequir 99, n. 90
ges 95
gilar 120
gilos 98, 120
ginolh 120
giquir 99
Giraut 120

gis 95
glatz 127
gra 56
gracia 68
grana 56
grans 84
Grec 76
guerra 28
guerriers 32

-id 119
ieu 85, 97
.il(l) 50, 56, 76
il(h) 36, 44
ilh (fem.) 94, 97
-ilh 44
ins 55
intrar 55
-ir 32
iraisser 126
.is 65
issam 98
issetz 121
issilh 97
issir 98
i(n)vern 64

ja 62, 103
jag 119
jai n. 73
jassempre n. 74
jassen n. 74
jatz n. 73
jauzion 85
jauzir 85
jazer 62
joglar 33, 99
joi 83
jorn 64, 120
juzeu 29

.l 56
l' 56
la(i) 50
lag 69
laida 69
laire 30
lait 69
lau n. 80
lausengiers 99
lauzas n. 80
lauzeta 83, 121

le(i)al 123
legresa 83
lei(s) 50, 86
leire 59
l(i)eu 43
lejal 123
.lh 76, 92
Lemotges 30
leng(u)a 46
leyal 123
li 43, 56
lial 123
lhun n. 38
loba 29
lo cals 72
logaditz 70
loindana 110
longamen(s) 96
longamentz 96
lop 29
lor 67, 90
lui 67
lums 116
lunh n. 38
lur 89

ma 67
ma(n) 26
maintas 113
maire 126
mais 36, 103
malapte 92
malaude 92
malaut(e) 91, 92
mals 112
man n. 68
mand 112
manda 122
mandas 59
mandat 60
mandei 59
mandes 59
man(h)tas 113
mar 19
marrir 77
marritz 77
mar (< magis) 36, n. 29
mas (< meas) 67
mases 35
medegar 48
medeis 87

meilz 41
meitatz 62
melher 27, 126
melhor 126
melor 36
membra 109
membre 109
mena 122
menatz 61
menor 126
menre 126
meravelha 85
maravilhas 85
merc 37
merces 94
mes 51
metat 62
meteis 87
meteisses 35
m(i)eu 29, 43
m(i)eus 29
mezeis 87
mi n. 85
mia 67, 68, 69
mi(g)a 103
midons 96, 99
mielhs 41
mieua 67, 68
miia 103
miralh 88
mis 55
mitat 62
mo(n) 103
moc 122
moler 36
molher 47
molt 60
mon (< monte) 31
mon (< mundu) 31, 42, 112
mori 64
moric 64
morit 64
mostrar 39
mot 60
moure 83
mout 60
mover 83
mult 26
muiller 47
mulher 47
mur 20

mur(s) 25

.N 47, 48
.n 52, 95
n' 71
naisser 104, 126
nasc 126
nasques 126
nau 20, 43, 92
naut 58
naveg 51
navei 51
navilli 46, 51
ne (< inde) 74
ne (< nec) 38
negre 127
neir 127
neps(a) 50
nes(s)a 50
neza 50
ni 38
nochs 118
noit 19, 118
noel 71
noire n. 34
nom 27, 28
nostres 111
nozer n. 34
nuech 118
nueit 19, 118
nu(i)l 43
nulh 43, 76
nuoch 118
nuoit 19, 118
nut 63

oblid' 84
oblidar 105
oc 18
olhs 88
oli 33
on 60
on(d)rar 74, 102
ora 19
orguoill 107
-os 116
ou 43

pabaillon 61
pabalhon 61
pagar 103
paiar 103

INDEX

palatz 104
par 92
paratges 111
pareis 92
pareiser 92
parer 92
parten 64
parti 64, 122
partic 64
partida 61
part(i)rai 95
partit (< parti(v)it) 64
partit (< partitu) 60
parven 107
pasmar 66
pasmes 66
paubra 70
pauc 83
pavilhon 61
pe 19
peier 27, 126
peira 20, 30
Peire 41
Peiro(n) 41
peiros 124
Peitau 31
pejor 126
pelicer 41
pels 42
penava 38
pen(d)re 74, n. 68
perd(i)ei 49, 65, 94
perd(i)est 65
perdet 77
perduda 61
perdut 60
persevera 122
p(r)estre 74
petit 86
piatat 65
pidat 65
pi(e)tat 65
plai 91, n. 73
planc 126
planh 126
planher 20, 104, 126
plassa 127
platz 84, n. 73
plazer 119
ploran 64
plus 44
poc 37, 51

poderos 116
podestat(z) 64
pogut 93
Poh 83
poi 83
pon 112
pon(d)re 74
porta 20
portel(a) 121
posc 86
pot 96
prada 56
prat 56
precs 96
preg 119
pregar 103
preiar 103
preiron 74
premiers 72
pren n. 68
prendre 74
preon 89
presta 46
pretz 104
pre(z)a 75
prezar 51, 104
prezeron 74
prion 89
pris 55
pro 86
proar 71
prodome 86
Proens(s)a 38, 71, 120
proes(s)a 71, 120
Proenza 38, 120
proeza 120
profech 89
prozome 86
prumier 72
pue(i)s n. 77
pui n. 99
pus (< plus) 44
pus (< post) 88, n. 77
puyar 94

quaitiu 31
que 27
quecs 107
querrai 95
ques 55
quet 68
q(u)ez 87

qui 27
quis 55

rag 119
rai 83, n. 99
raizo 51
rancor 102
rancur(a) 102
raso(n) 50
raubar 75
raubet 75
rauja 62
razo 68
razos 66
re(n) 30, 103
re(i)alme 72
receubut(z) 68
receup 62, 68
receuput 68
receuta n. 60
recreire 97
rege(s)me 72
regisme 72
remairon 74
remanc 127
remanh 126
rema(n)seron 74
remazeron 74
remazon 74
ren (< rendo) 67
rendes 123
re(i)ssidar 119
retraire 92
Richart 31
rics 110
roda 19
rog(e) 34
romput 60
rotz 60
rouge n. 99

.s 65
sa 67
sa(i) 50
sabde 91
saber 20, 29, 34, 58
sachatz 62
sacrifici 56
sai 86
saizo 51
salhir 63
salvatges 112

sapchatz 62
sapiatz 62
sapte 91
sas 67
saub 58, 68
saubem 58
saubi 94
saubist 58
saup 34, 58, 62, n. 27
saupron 74
savis 33, 34
se 35
segon 125
sejornar 125
selhuy 45
semblar 49
sen 62
senas 124
senhal 98, 99
senher 27
senhor 27
senhors 117
serai 102
sercar 43
sert 43
servizi 56
ses 96, 124
sidons 96
s(i)eus 29
si 35
sia 67
sieu 68
sieua 68
sirventes 38, 39
so 43
so(n) (< sum) 93, 103
so(n) (<suum) 30
soa 68, 69
soau 118
soi 93
sojorn 125
sojornar 125
soldader 69
solh 90
solt 69
som 68
son 68
sonar 49
sorger 45
sorzer 45
sotil 91
sotz 91

soudadier 69
soudadiers 69
sua 69
suau 118
suelh 90
sui 93
su(z)or 75

ta 67
tailla 46
tal 19
tan(t) 112
tas 67
te(n) 90
tela 19
temps 28
tenc (< teneo) 126, 127
tenc (< tenuit) 28, 34
tenguist 28, 34
ten(d)re 102
t(i)eus 29
tengut 93
tenh 126, 127
tezaur 19, 75
tieu 68
tieua 68
toa 68, 69
tolc 88
tolgut 87, 93
tol(d)re 102
totz 28
tout 87
touta 77
trac 92
tractar 34
trahia 104
trai (< tragit) 90
trai (< trago) 92
traïda 75, 104
traire 59
trau 92
trazida 104
tregua 38
trei 75
tresor 75
treva 38
tro 125, n. 112
trobador 33
trobaire 20, 33
trobar 33
tua 68, 69
tuch 76, n. 69

tug 76
tuoilla 108
tu(i)t 36, n. 69

Uc 48, 92
U(c)s 48
uelhs 88
ueu 43
ultra 26
uou 43
u(i)s 86
u(n)s 26
.us 62
uvern 73

vai 84
val 28, 104
valc 37
valens 64
valgut 93
valor 19
va(i)r 36
vas 104
vau 97
ve(n) 85
vei 63, 83
velhatz 118
venc 37
venca 107
vencut 107
venderon 74
vendet 65, 77
vendetz 121
vendon 60
venguda 118
vengut 93
venh 126
venquei 107
venser 20, 107
venssa 107
ver 116
verai 42, 116
veraia 116
vers 42
ve(r)s 104
ves(z)com(p)s 28, 30
ves(z)com(p)te 28, 30
vescont 30
vesque n. 14
vetz 35, 119
veya 85
vezer 20, 38

INDEX 139

vezets 121
vezi(s) 30, 119
vezon 60
vi 105, n. 94
via 27, 67, 77
viatge 111
vida 20
viron 74
viure 83
v(u)oill 109
vol 109
volc 37
volen 88
volentat 88
volentier 88
volgra 126
volia 35
volon 88
volontat 88
volontier 88
volrai 95
volria 102
vostres 122
votz 35, 119
vuoilla 109

zel 120
Zili 45, 46

French

-age n. 99
aidier 117
ainc n. 67
ainsi 89
ainz 106, n. 77
aise 110
aissi 89
aju 117
aller 49, n. 49
amie 20
as 42
aurai 87
autrui 45
avenant 105
avoir 19
ayant 64

bocage 120
bourg 74
brasse 127

celui 45
cestui 45
chanta 46
chantant 64
chanteve 38
chantez 121
Charles 31
châsse 87
chauffard 69
chétif 96
chevaliers 32
chevauchons 123
chèvre 19
Chypre 50
cil 44
cinq 68
cist 44
coi 68
comme 39
conforter 105
coude 91
coute 91
cria 66
cropeton 123
Cypre 50

dame 89
déplaît 109
dérober 76
des 42
devoir 76
dieu 29
disant 64
dist 45
divenres 64
dormillous 124
douce 84
douter 91

embrasser 127
encore 73
ensi 89
enveer 77
envir(i)e 46
ere 35
er(e)t 34
esteie 35
évêché 26
exil n. 88

faible 92
faimes 122

faisons 121
fait n. 28
faites 122
famille n. 88
femme 89
feuille 56
fils 37
fin 111, 112
forcené 62
fors 124
forsener 62
fueil 56
fui 26

garir 48
genouillons 123
gentil 112
gentilhomme 112
Gilles 45, 46
Gires 45, 46
grâce 68
grain(e) 56
grammaire 46
guérir 48

heretaige 57
heriter 57
heure 19
hiver 64
huis 86

iere 35
ier(e)t 34
il 36
ist n. 6, n. 88

ja 103
jaloux 120
joie 83
jongleur 33
jouir 85
jour 64

lait n. 28
larme 48
lerme 48
li 43
loeis 70
loyal 124

marri 77
Mathieu 29

meie 67
mer 19
merveille 85
mienne 67
mirail 88
mire 46
moie 67
mon n. 85
monsieur n. 85
mont 42
montrer 39
mouvoir 83
mur 20

naïf 104
navie 51
navilie 51
navir(i)e 51
nelui 45
nos 111
nouvel 71
nuit n. 6
nului 45

ont 113
or 19
or(e) 125
orgueil 107
ouaille 71

pâmer 66
paon 31
paraît 92
paraître 92
paroir 92
partant 64
paveillon 61
pelletier 41
perdiet 49
pert 92
peur 31
pied 19
pigeon n. 26
pillard 69
porte 20
printemps 72
profit 89
prouver 71
prud'homme 86
puis n. 77

raison 68

rancune 102, n. 91
rancure 102
réal 124
reculons 122
régime 72
remire 46
robe 75
rompu 60
rot 60
route 60
royal 124
royaume 72

sache 34
sage 34, n. 26
saillir 63
savoir 20
seigneur 27
séjourner 125
sembler 49
semondre 89
sens 62
sire 27
six n. 6
soef 118
soldat 69
soldee 69
solde(i)er 69
soldier 69
soldoier 69
sou 69
soudart 69

tâtons 123
tel 19
toile 19
tout 87
trahir 104
trésor 19
trêve 38
trive 38
trouver 33
trouvère 33
tuit n. 69

valeur 19
veillez 118
veir 116
vendez 121
vendiet 49
vendredi 64
ventrillons 123

vice-consul 30
vicomte 30
vidame 30
vie 20
voie 27, 77
voir 116
voisins 30
voix 35
voyez 121
vrai 42

zèle 120

Italian

-aggio n. 99
aitiamo 117
aiuto 117
altrui 45
anche n. 67
ancora 73
andare n. 49
andiede 49
assagiare 120

bevuto 93
bocconi 123
borgo 74

caduto 93
cantò 46
chiesto 52
cinque 68
Cipro 50
coglie 109
cogliere 108
colga 109
come 39
confortare 105
coraggio n. 99

desse 123
destare 119
detto 55
dolve 107
dovere 76

fare 39
fidare 90
fino 111
foglia 56

INDEX 141

foglio 56
foste 26
fosti 26
franco 108
fu 26
fui 26
fummo 26
furono 26

ginocchioni 123
giorno 64
godere 85

insieme n. 31
inverno 64

meravegia 85
meraviglia 85
messi 51
missi 51
muovere 83

parvente 107
parvenza 107
parvi 107
penzoloni 123
piede 19

rancore 102
rimagno n. 116
rimango n. 116
resedarse 119
roba 76
rubare 76
ruota 19

saggio 120
senno 62
senso 62

tegno n. 116
tengo n. 116
tregua 38

vantaggio n. 99
veduto 93
vegno n. 116
vengo n. 116
via 27

ženero 46

ženta 46
ženu 46
žənuju 46

Spanish

abrazar 127
agora 125, n. 113
-aje n. 99
amiga 20
andar n. 49

braza 127

caja 87
cantad 121, n. 105
cantáis n. 105
cantó 46
cinco 68
confortar 105
cuñado 47

delante 125
diese 123
dormijoso 124
dudar 91

ensayar 120
ensiemo n. 31
escucha n. 6

franco 108

hecho n. 28
heredar 57
hombre 109

jugar 45

leche n. 34
lugar 45

mas n. 29
mujer 47

orgüello n. 95
orgullo n. 95
oír n. 44

pabellón 61
pichón n. 26
pié 19
poco 120
poderoso 116

quedo 68
quién 30

ramaje n. 99
redondo 89
rencor 102
rencura 102
rueda 19

saber 20
salir 63
salvaje n. 99
soldadero 69
sope n. 27
sudor n. 44
supe n. 27

tengo n. 116
tregua 38

vecinos 30
ved 121
vended 121
vengo n. 116
verdadero 116
verso 104
vía 27
vida 20
viesso 104

ya 103

Portuguese

amiga 20
caixa 87
cantou 46
confortar 105
desse 123
escuta n. 6
feito n. 28
franco 108
houve n. 27
leite n. 28
pé 19

poderoso 116
preceuto n. 60
quedo 68
rancura 102
roda 19
saber 20
soube n. 27
tenho n. 116
venho n. 116

via 27
vida 20

Catalan

adenant 125
anar n. 49
confortar 105

eix 87
enant 125
goig n. 71
mas n. 29
or n. 71
orgull n. 95
poc n. 95
ull n. 95

The Department of Romance Studies Digital Arts and Collaboration Lab at the University of North Carolina at Chapel Hill is proud to support the digitization of the North Carolina Studies in the Romance Languages and Literatures series.

www.ingramcontent.com/pod-product-compliance
Lightning Source LLC
Chambersburg PA
CBHW020419230426
43663CB00007BA/1229